THAT RACE

STAWELL '96 – 15 INSPIRING STORIES

David Griffin

Published by Wilkinson Publishing Pty Ltd
ACN 006 042 173
PO Box 24135, Melbourne, VIC 3001, Australia.
Ph: +61 3 9654 5446
enquiries@wilkinsonpublishing.com.au
www.wilkinsonpublishing.com.au

Copyright © 2026 David Griffin.

WilkinsonPublishing
wilkinsonpublishinghouse

All rights reserved. No part of this publication may be reproduced, stored in a retrieval system or transmitted in any form by any means without the prior permission of the copyright owner. Enquiries should be made to the publisher.
Every effort has been made to ensure that this book is free from error or omissions. However, the Publisher, the Authors, the Editor or their respective employees or agents, shall not accept responsibility for injury, loss or damage occasioned to any person acting or refraining from action as a result of material in this book whether or not such injury, loss or damage is in any way due to any negligent act or omission, breach of duty or default on the part of the Publisher, the Authors, the Editor, or their respective employees or agents.

Title: That Race
ISBN: 9781923259188
A catalogue record of this book is available from the National Library of Australia.

Design by Michael Bannenberg.
Printed and bound in Australia by Ligare.

Photographs of the 1996 Stawell Gift - Mark Dadswell.
Reproduction permission - the Dadswell family.
All other photographs sourced from private collections and the AFL.

CONTENTS

Wilkinson Publishing acknowledges the Traditional Owners of the Country on which we work and reside, the Wurundjeri Woiwurrung People of the Kulin Nation and recognises their continuing connection to the land, waters and culture. We pay our respects to their Elders past and present and extend that acknowledgment to Traditional Owners across Australia.

Foreword
Lord Sebastian Coe

Cathy Freeman and the Stawell Gift are both icons of Australian sport, and beyond. Their history is intertwined.

After her two wins at Stawell – in 1995 and 1996 – Freeman became one of the greatest 400m athletes in history, winning Olympic and world titles.

Another four years on, Freeman became Olympic champion on home soil in Sydney. I was in the Stadium that night, working with Channel 7, and can still see and hear the 112,000 screaming fans who followed Cathy's every stride around that 400m track.

This year marks the 30th anniversary of Freeman's second 400m win – one of the most memorable races ever witnessed at Stawell, an event that was awarded a World Athletics Heritage Plaque in 2019.

Steeped in history, the Stawell Gift uniquely features races run on grass in which athletes start off varying marks according to form and ability. It's a meeting like no other and it's been part of the Australian athletics scene since 1878.

In 1996, Freeman started some 40 metres behind but ran down the leaders to win in 50.54 seconds. Just three months later, she placed a brilliant second to the great Marie-José Pérec in the Atlanta Olympic 400m final. Another four years on, Freeman became Olympic champion on home soil in Sydney.

That Race celebrates not only Stawell and Freeman but also the six other women who competed against her.

While it is a celebration of women and athletics, it also reflects the broader spirit of sport.

I hope you enjoy *That Race*.

David Griffin – My Story.

I started writing this book over 14 years ago. I met a gentleman by the name of William Hadlow at the boxing one evening. He had just lost a bruising encounter for the Australian Middleweight title. I came to learn that Hadlow was a better fighter than he was a boxer.

That Race is a collection of biographical short stories and interviews, from a broad range of sports people. Some of the subjects are well known, others aren't, but what it examines, is the spectrum of human characteristics, emotions, passion, and resilience. In uncovering the stories, we learn about terrorism, our indigenous history, different cultures, people and the quirkiness of human nature.

Each non-fiction tale explores significant moments and, unlike most sports books, the on-field action takes a back seat to the focus on life and emotion. Most of the interviews highlight what happened outside the ground, oval, ring or track.

Some stories take place around Cathy Freemans win in the 1996 Stawell 400 metres, whilst others, are more metaphorical, but no less impactful.

It's worth noting that no AI was used in the writing any of the stories. The interviews and stories were done the hard way and included blood, sweat and lots of tears.

I am 56 years old now and I remember growing up in the 1970s. It feels like yesterday.

I grew up in Shepparton in central Victoria. As a kid, I was small and I smiled a lot. My brown hair always seemed to be messy. I have photos to prove it.

I lived in shorts and sneakers and I fixated on sport 12 months of the year. It was more important than school. I guess that was normal for a country kid.

I loved most sports but I can't ever recall not thinking about football. Ever. There was a time when all I could dream about was running out onto the MCG on Grand Final Day.

As a kid, I kicked the football in the backyard, the front yard, at the park and in the hallways around my house – much to mum's annoyance! When an actual football was nowhere to be found, I kicked whatever I could find. Socks wrapped tightly together, inflated balloons, pillows, and cushions. All good makeshift footballs if you ask me.

I ran around the house kicking goals through doors and taking great marks over the lounge chairs. I was always the hero, of course. My fantasy was kicking bags of goals and winning games with a kick after the siren.

I dreamt of playing for the St Kilda Football Club. I can thank my grandad for that. The Saints were his team.

I spent a lot of time with grandad as a kid. He talked to me like I was grown up for some reason. I was his first-born grandchild, so in many ways, I was spoiled.

I'm sure grandad said I could be a footballer one day. I can't remember him saying it, but I guess he did. He was like that. Grandad was also into horses. He loved trotters. Our family trained them. We didn't win much though.

I remember times when my grandad would sit with me in his backyard. Me crouched over an old-worn football, watching him tinkering with his trotting gear.

We sat together and listened to the football on the transistor radio. In the late seventies, the Saints weren't that good, so we didn't get to hear them very often. They were rarely the highlighted game of the day. We got random scores when they went "around the grounds" and the likes of Kevin "Skeeter" Coghlan reported from some far-flung oval in the big smoke. Normally the Saints were falling further behind. I cared a lot, and wins were rare in the ocean of loses.

The radio games seemed so far away. On another planet even. It was like a movie, and I dreamt about playing in a radio game. Trevor Barker was my hero, but there were others. Jeff Dunne, Bruce Duperouzal, Jeff Sarua and the like of Greg Burns and Jeff "Joffa" Cunningham later on.

I later played against Joffa at VFL level. He was old then, but still as tough as teak and he knew how to get the footy.

Grandad used to wear a type of fedora hat. It made him look distinguished. I was later to learn he wore it to cover his bald head.

It was the 70s and things were different. It was a time where smartphones, social media, the internet, wifi and laptops were still 30 years away.

Technology in the 70s was a black and white television, that was soon to go to colour. Television sets were clunky big blocks of wires and tubes, and all TV stations went off the air at midnight and came back on at 6am. No 24 hour TV in those days. Try searching for the test pattern on YouTube and you will see what I mean.

Phones were connected to a wall with a cord. Cars were different as well. You changed gears manually with a clutch. There was no air conditioning either. You had to wind the windows down with a handle to get any air. On hot days in summer, the plastic vinyl seats gave you 2nd degree burns and if your skin touched the metal seat belt buckles, then you were hospital bound.

We drank water straight from the garden hose, built cubby houses, went yabbying and swung on the Hills Hoist clothes lines, until we bent the metal arms and got in trouble. It was a good time.

I was an avid reader as well. I loved words. I love the places that words took me and the tales they told. Books like the *Magic Faraway Tree*, *The Secret Seven*, *James and the Giant Peach*, *Fantastic Mr Fox* and *Danny the Champion of the World* were some of my favourites. Enid Blyton and Roald Dahl were authors that spoke to me. You could feel the tales they told and the words they stitched together were like comfortable blankets that enveloped you, keeping you safe and warm.

I met a real author when I was about eight years old. Christobel Mattingley was a children's author who visited my school on a weekend. I bought one of her books and she signed it. She was larger than life and equal to any VFL(AFL) player that I admired. I wanted to be an author from that moment on.

I managed to play senior football as junior player. My home club was Shepparton United.

I went to University in Bendigo and I played footy with South Bendigo, coached by former Essendon premiership player Peter Bradbury. The Bendigo league was one of the best in Country Victoria. I was studying Nursing at Latrobe University. We won a couple of premierships. I consider myself very lucky.

I spent my youth wanting to play AFL football, I actually got close, when I was drafted to Sydney in 1990 at pick 67. I was chosen ahead of James Hird. That's my claim to fame. He was pick 79.

Between Hird and myself, we played 253 games, won a Brownlow medal, a Norm Smith medal and won two premierships. Of course I'm being tongue-in-cheek, because I played exactly zero games.

But as quickly as my career began, it ended. I was sacked from Sydney in 1991 almost at the start of the season, having played a couple of reserves games.

Whilst lamenting the fact I wasn't going to play professional Aussie Rules, I decided to travel overseas and ended up racing at the famous Powderhall Gift in Scotland. I remember introducing myself to the great Scottish Stawell Gift winner Goerge McNeil, in the changerooms at the Meadowbank stadium in Edinburgh, who in turn, introduced me to his trainer Bert Logan.

Bert was a well known bookmaker, runner and had coached a few athletes over his time. Bert kindly took me into the fold, and I trained with them in the lead up to the Gift. They were good days and gave me an international view of professional athletics.

Once through the Scottish experiment, I moved to County Wexford in Ireland and played Gaelic football with a small team called Glynn Barntown.

They played in the top division in the county. I lived in a pub and bluffed my way into a job as a gym instructor of a hotel gymnasium. God only knows how I did that.

Playing in Ireland was almost comedic. My very first game was classic TV ringside, but without Ron Casey commentating. A red-haired Irishman took exception to what might have been a bump and proceeded to hit me with every punch he threw. Hooks, uppercuts, lefts and rights, he threw everything at me and, most of them landed flush on my head.

My welcome to Gaelic football was blunt and painful. Through swollen eyes, I struggled to see out the remainder of the game.

On return to Australia I played for VFL Club Box Hill and ended up coaching junior football in the Eastern suburbs of Melbourne. I even had a couple of years coaching women's football.

I had experience as a runner with AFL clubs Sydney and Hawthorn. I was working with the sport brand Puma and living in Sydney at the time of the 2000 Olympics.

I was overseeing the Puma brand partnership with the Sydney Swans and they needed a runner – someone to run messages for the coaching staff. I started with the reserves and then worked with

Rodney "Rocket" Eade as senior runner.

Sometimes Rocket's passion would spill over during a game and I will forever remember him grabbing me by the scruff of the neck during a practice match, because of something I did or didn't do. He was a stickler for protocols, and outside the game of footy, he is a good guy.

A highlight of my sporting career (albeit by 'association') was doing the running for the Hawks 2008 premiership season. I was runner for 2007, 2008 and the start of the 2009 seasons. An AFL premiership is amazing. I was in the right place at the right time and very lucky to experience it.

It was cathartic being at Hawthorn. After being sacked from Sydney as a player, to be amongst greats like Luke Hodge, Sam Mitchell and Cyril Rioli, it was very clear I wasn't that good as a player. Seeing the best up close, was cleansing and good for me. It was a salient reminder that my talents lay elsewhere.

As a boy, I dreamt of running out on the MCG on Grand Final Day. I used to imagine what the crowd would be like. 100,000 strong, screaming. Maybe my dream actually did come true, albeit, as a runner.

I decided to try professional athletics to get fit in the off season for football. I was a former little athlete so it made sense. Professional athletics and the Stawell Gift become a goal. Not the Gift itself mind you. I was more of a 400 metre runner.

I started training with former 1964 Stawell Gift winner Noel Hussey in Shepparton. Noel was the sports editor of the local paper and quite the personality.

There was an issue though, and it had to do with my speed. I didn't have much of it. That's not a good thing in a sport like running. So I didn't ascend the heights of the greats, but I really enjoyed it and I am still competing in professional athletics as a 56 year old. The body takes a while to recover though, and I'm constantly sore, but I love it.

The stories of people have always fascinated me. I self-published two books and donated all proceeds of the books to charity. *Everyday Heroes* and *A Journey So Far* were published through Croxton House and we donated close to $80,000.

I was also involved in the production of two documentaries. *The Spirit of Boxing* was launched through cinema, and *Max Bailey Premiership Player* was released on Fox Sports.

Much like *That Race*, the books and films tell the story of unique individuals.

I commenced this book journey in 2012. It was around that time that I interviewed boxer William Hadlow on the Gold coast. I saw William fight in Melbourne.

He was brave and his courage astounded me. He was defiant in the face of great odds and an African with a chiseled body that towered over him. William kept moving forward under a barrage of punches. He didn't take a backward step. He lost the fight, but won the crowd.

Hadlow became the face of this project and I wanted to tell his story, a beautiful tale of perseverance and triumph, but not necessarily sporting glory.

Over the journey I met many different people. People that left an impression on me. That's what this book is – a collection of stories of people running in their own race. Centered on sport, most of the stories are focused off field.

In many ways *That Race* is centered on a specific race; the famous Cathy Freeman 400 metre victory at the Stawell Gift in 1996, but it's also about another six women in that race, in addition to another eight people from various sports, who have had to run their own race.

Shanie Singleton finished second to Cathy Freeman in the 1996 Stawell 400 metres but became more well-known because of her loss, rather than the potential of the win.

Third-placegetter Tara Gleason went on to be a very successful Victorian athletic league runner.

Jackie Chehade finished fourth and became 'Youtube famous' for elbowing Freeman as she went past her 60 metres from the finish line.

Emma Yeomans, who was pipped by Chehade and came fifth, was in the stands crying as she watched Freeman win the 400 gold medal at the Sydney Olympics four years later.

Sixth-placegetter, 19-year-old Kim McDonough's father was born in Stawell. She was the youngest in the field and it was her first Stawell Gift final.

In seventh position was mother of two, Deb Tomsett who at 38 was the oldest in the field.

An interesting side note was the fact the six finalists in the race all married within the professional athletic ranks.

Just as important and all running in their own race, we have included eight other stories from various sports.

William Hadlow survived the horrors of foster care in Queensland. Boxing for Hadlow was easy, compared to his childhood.

Tim and David Clarke were AFL brothers. Tim was with the

Hawks and David played with Geelong and Carlton. The sons of a VFL legend, both boys were innocent bystanders in terrorist attacks at different times.

Max Bailey is a Hawthorn football club premiership player who endured three knee reconstructions.

Charlene Rendina and others saw first hand the horrors of the terrorist attacks at the 1972 Munich Olympics.

Susie Ramadan is a female on a mission. The diminutive Muslim boxer has defied the odds to be one of Australia's best female fighters ever.

World champion powerlifter Ross Knight lives in the back blocks of country Victoria. His band the Cosmic Psychos has opened for Pearl Jam, and he counts Eddie Vedder as one of his closest friends.

Tom Deanne and Goldie Heath grew up in a time when you could make a quid by sprinting. Both teamed up for the first Stawell Gift win after the second world war and found a unique spot to train away from the public gaze.

Western Bulldogs board member Belinda Duarte is a direct descendant of Robert Kinnear, the first indigenous winner of the Stawell Gift. Duarte talks about life in Australia.

I have found that in most instances, what happens away from the sporting arena (large or small) is far more interesting than what happens on it.

That Race is about life and what it takes to overcome adversity and hardships along the way. It is a celebration of humanity and one I hope will both entertain and enlighten.

I need to give thanks to multiple people for help and assistance in this project. First goes to Micheal Wilkinson at Wilkinson publishing, for his belief in the project. His assistance and nurturing, to get through the last couple of months was a key to it taking shape.

I need to thank my kids, Tom and Sophie. They are starting on their own path and I look forward to seeing where life takes them.

My brother Glen and sister Christine have been unwavering in support of me and anything I have done. We are three vastly different people, and whilst I am sure they look at me, roll their eyes and wonder how I came to be so different, they keep fronting up as only awesome siblings can.

Nick Karandonis in Sydney has also been resolute in his support of not only this project but me personally over the past 15 odd years. His support of my writing and his balanced feedback has been welcomed.

As far as writing goes, I also need to acknowledge author David Metzenthen who over the years gave me great support and feedback. A subject of one of my earlier books, David writes as well as anybody in the business.

Jon Anderson and the late great John Forbes gave me the confidence to continue to write. 'Chipping away' has been a forte supported by both.

Brad Armstong has also been a good friend throughout the process and Damien Horne is another I want to acknowledge.

Jon Anderson

Melbourne *Herald Sun* Journalist, Jon Anderson has been writing about sport for over 40 years. The 69 year old has seen the best in most sports, come and go.

He cut his teeth with renowned scribe Scott Palmer at the *Sunday Press* in the 80s, and has been writing about sport for what seems like forever.

He loved athletics but says he wasn't much of a runner himself. It was the test of pure athletic endeavor that impressed him. It was raw, man against man, woman against woman.

He wouldn't have a clue how many world-class sports people he has interviewed. He doesn't much care about that type of thing. He's not easily impressed, and it makes what he says about Cathy Freeman significant.

"Ando" as he's known, can recite great sporting performances, dates and times with ease, and he has a well-informed view on sportspeople from different eras. The "who's better" argument is a never-ending one in a pub, and I would back Ando in any sports debate.

His favorite athletes were Ron Clarke and Raelene Boyle. Clarke won bronze in the 10,000 metres at the Tokyo Olympics in 1964, and Boyle should have won three Olympic gold medals if it wasn't for the Russians.

Anderson knows a lot about professional athletics. He has been a regular visitor to the Stawell Gift and he reported on Freemans 1996 win for the Herald Sun. Both his sons have won professional races, with his eldest Jack winning the prestigious 400 metre back markers at Stawell.

For Anderson, Cathy Freeman has been Australia's best-ever athlete. Full stop.

"Having won 41 of 42 races straight, at the peak of her career, no other Australian athlete has done that on the international stage," he said.

"The only other athlete I could compare her to is Herb Elliot, who was never beaten over the mile or 1500 metres. Apologies must also go to Betty Cuthbert who won a 100/200 double at the Melbourne Olympics in 1956 and eight years later came back and won the 400 metres at Tokyo, which is remarkable" he added.

Anderson first met Freeman in the early 90s when he was working with her then manager Nick Bideau.

"Whilst on the surface she was shy, a bit giggly and nervous, underneath there was this steely determination and people underestimated her. She was a tough competitor and had amazing self-belief."

"She is the golden child of Australian sprinting. Everybody knows who she is."

He saw both her 1995 and 1996, 400 metre Stawell wins. The 1996 win is arguably the best race ever seen at the Stawell Gift across all distances and was a springboard for an assault on the Atlanta 400 Olympic title three months later.

Anderson felt Freeman's Stawell 400 metre win in 1996, sat comfortably in the top three races she's run and wasn't out of place alongside her Sydney Olympic Games Gold and her Silver medal from Atlanta.

Her 1996 Stawell 400 metre win was the perfect preparation for an assault on the Atlanta Olympics to be held in July, only three months after her magnificent effort on the grass track.

Anderson wrote an article for the *Herald Sun* in 2014 that sums the race up.

For any religious Freeman watcher, and my vicarious journey began in 1990 at the Auckland Commonwealth Games, what she achieved at Stawell on Easter Monday, 1996, sits comfortably alongside her finest. Or the finest of any Australian athlete, anywhere, anytime.

In early 1996 most Australians were unsure just how good she was, aware of her 200m-400m double at the 1994 Commonwealth Games in Canada but also aware that the Commonwealth Games was a long way short of Olympic level. And that was what Freeman was targeting in 1996, the Atlanta Olympics falling just three months after Stawell where she had entered the women's 400m and conceded up to 42 metres under the handicap conditions.

On the Sunday night prior to the race she relaxed with then boyfriend and manager Nic Bideau. Never a big drinker, Freeman decided to prepare for the next day with a glass of 1994 Summerfield Shiraz, a vintage that met with her approval.

Being able to switch off away from the track was an asset throughout her career because once on it she became one of the most single-minded athletes in the world, allowing nothing to penetrate her target.

For the first 15 seconds of the TV coverage you can't see Freeman before her distinctive long, fluent stride comes into picture.

She then disappears for a further 10 seconds as the battlers do their bit, then it becomes seriously interesting when she starts to hunt the rabbits. She passes a runner then another runner appears to lash out with her elbow as Freeman powers past.

It could have unsettled a lesser athlete, indeed 500kg thoroughbreds have spat the dummy for similar, but not this girl. Within 10 strides she has passed four more, runners who appear to be going up and down on the spot. Then with one last desperate lunge she passes the final figure, clocking a time of 50.48sec.

For the uneducated that time on a grass track, in a race where you need to run wide to avoid the flotsam, is the rough equivalent of 49 seconds flat on a normal track. To me that is as good as it gets.

Freeman, prone to short sentences and understatement, even surprised herself although there was little time to savour the moment given she had to catch a flight for the US to begin her Olympic preparation. That would lead to a career best of 48.63 in running second to leggy Frenchwoman Marie-Jose Perec (48.25) at the Atlanta Olympics.

She would never lose to Perec again and but for injury at Oslow in 1998 would have gone undefeated between Stawell and her 2000 Sydney Olympic gold medal. That is hard to comprehend today, or ever, an Australian track athlete ruling the world for four years.

Her race, in an event that was first run by gold miners in Stawell for a bit of fun back in the 1800s, captures everything we love in our country.

When athletics afficionados speak of great races at the Stawell Gift they generally speak of the famous run of Jean Louis

Ravelomanantsoa, who won the Gift off scratch in 1975.

Another great run was that of Josh Ross who won the 120 metre Gift from the scratch mark in 2005.

Cathy Freeman has been the only winner to win the 400 metres from scratch and many see her win as the best race ever seen at the Stawell Gift.

For Jon Anderson the equation is a simple one:

"Cathy Freeman is an icon of Australian sport and sporting success. Everybody knows about her and I think there should be a class at school that teaches all kids about Cathy Freeman. It's a great story and one in which should be told and retold."

Australia Post
Aust
Gatorade

1ST Cathy Freeman

"I have always relished an opportunity to compete, although I could always leave it on the track. If I got beaten, it's fair and square. The Stawell Gift of '96 I had to really work hard. I have never been pushed, like I was that day at Stawell. I had to earn it, and I give respect to the girls and those around who enabled that opportunity."

Cathy Freeman stood on the starting line. With very little emotion, she kicked her legs out, either through nervousness, habit, or maybe she was just trying to keep warm. It was a cold day.

She had been here before, last year in fact, and had won easily. This was the 1996 Stawell Gift women's 400 metre final. The seconds ticked by and she waited.

The race wasn't at some beautifully crafted athletic stadium, in some far-flung cushy meeting in Europe, it was at a venue that was far more important than that. A unique, picturesque, grass football oval, in the small western Victorian country town, and a meeting that was first run in 1878.

Sequential photographs of 'That Race' are from the proof sheet of photographer Mark Dadswell.

She also wasn't amongst the worlds' elite runners either, she was here with mums and part timers, for whom this was the Olympics, and the highlight of the year.

With an appealing community feel, professional foot running is for everybody, that is, if you're prepared to do the work. It accepts all that come, irrespective of colour, race, sexual orientation or occupation. If you can run and you are prepared to do the work, this sport welcomes you. Cathy Freeman loved it because of that.

Every Easter the television crews crawl over central park like ants, setting up sophisticated, expensive equipment, that looked well out of place amongst the rustic confines of the football oval that plays host. It's only when the likes of legendary commentator Bruce MacAvaney walk amongst the crowd, do the part timers of the pro scene, feel that they are part of something special.

You can hear the cockies and crows screech in the background and, every couple of hours, the rhythmic hum and clunk of trains can be heard as they pull into the Stawell Station, less than 100 metres away. It is a station as old as the athletic meeting itself. 10,000 people stood shoulder to shoulder, packed in like sardines around the tiny oval. All eyes were on the reigning

Commonwealth Games gold medallist.

Freeman was a star on the rise. History says she sits easily amongst the best athletes Australia has ever produced. Celebrated and lauded as one of the best, it started here, in Stawell, a whistle stop on the drive from Melbourne to Adelaide.

She stood barely five metres from the crowd and waited. A far cry from the Commonwealth and Olympics Games where the crowd and athletes were never to meet. On the world scene, the superstars of the track are a well-protected commodity.

The smell of sizzling BBQs wafted across the track. The unmistakeable aroma of oil, sausages and burnt onions, hung in the cold air.

Her name was whispered in hushed tones all around the track. Muffled and secretive, the punters talked about her chances. Surely she couldn't win from that far back they surmised. It can't be done, she's too far back.

Wearing the red colour that signifies the backmarker in a professional race, she wore black shorts and surprisingly, sunglasses. She was elegant, fit, and looked every bit the professional athlete.

The whistle sounded to get on their marks. Whistles replace starters orders in circular track Professional athletics events. It's historical and it's been that way forever.

With the first whistle she got to the line. She was in a standing start, not typical of a 400 metre sprint and different from her 1995 win, where she started in the crouch position.

The second whistle goes and she is set. The gun blasts and she was off. A collective gasp reverberated around the little oval. Nobody knew what was about to happen, not the crowd, not the other runners in the race, not Cathy herself.

She took off at pace. There was to be no relaxing in this race. I was to learn that when Cathy Freeman runs she always runs hard. Her wonderful, easy-going demeanour belies the fact that she is a super competitor and has an innate urge to always run to her best.

I met Cathy at a café in the Melbourne Suburb of Elwood. It was school holidays and she said she had been held hostage by her 14-year-old daughter Ruby. School holidays can be tough.

Her toothy smile makes you feel welcome and it's almost like we are old friends. It's nice.

I was surprised that she wanted to know more about me. Did I

have kids? Where did I work? What have I done before?

We spoke for an hour about life. It was delightful. Now a YouTube favourite, she looks back at that race as one of her best ever.

"I loved that race. My favourite race is a toss up between Stawell and Atlanta," she said.

The contrast between the intensity of the Atlanta Olympic venue, that held 100,000 people and this quant country Victorian meeting, wasn't lost on me.

"Most people think that Sydney must be my favourite race but it's not. I ran fast in Atlanta, and yes I was beaten by a super runner in Marie Jose Perec, but the time of 48.63 seconds made it better than Sydney," she said.

"Stawell was also a happy place for me. It was my favourite race in terms of the challenge. Sydney isn't. It's either Atlanta or Stawell as my favourite race."

Cathy Freeman sits at number 11 on the all time list for the fastest female 400 metre runners ever. Her time of 48.63 seconds is an Australian record. It earned her a silver medal at the Atlanta Olympics.

It was the Commonwealth Games in Victoria Canada, in 1994,

that proved to be her unveiling. Winning the 400 and 200 metre double, she announced to the world that she was a class athlete.

53 year old Freeman finished her career with a CV as good as anyone's in world sprinting history:

- 2000 Sydney Olympics 400 metres gold medal.
- 1996 Atlanta Olympics 400 metres silver medal.
- 1997 Athens World Championships 400 metres gold medal.
- 1999 Seville World championship 400 metres gold medal.

Add that to her other four gold medals at the Commonwealth games across 200 metres, 400 metres and the relays, and Freeman sits in rare company.

At the age of 16, she was also the first female indigenous athlete to win a Commonwealth Games Gold Medal.

For many she is the pin-up girl of Aussie athletics, and whilst she was at home on the perfectly flat tartan tracks of Europe, she was just as happy running on the football ovals of country towns around Australia.

"In the lead up to Stawell I had been running in the Tasmania Gift circuit. All of these gifts are held on grass and I think I

started to get used to it. I loved running on grass and it showed at Stawell. The fact that the spikes are long and you have to really work and dig in and get some great traction, my body liked that."

"In reality I think I just loved running. Running was where I felt happiest. And I really liked handicap running."

It's her easy-going nature that people are attracted to. What you see is what you get with Freeman, and she felt at home with the country folk of the professional running scene.

"Pro running in the country felt like you were in the middle of nowhere and it was a simple, slow country vibe that I liked. I'm from the country and I have an affinity with the characters and down to earth people."

She remembers Stawell and the weekend clearly, the race less so, but when you have run as many 400 metre races as Cathy, she can be forgiven.

"I remember a lot of things. I had a red wine the night before the final. I don't normally have red wine but it was nice. Maybe it helped me relax?"

"As far as the race itself, I remember getting to the start line and I couldn't see some of the runners up ahead. The shape of the ground isn't an oval, and you get sort of disorientated and don't

insulco
1
STRIPROLL
ROOFING PRODUCTS

really know how much of the race is left. On a tartan athletics track you know where you are all the time, and you can pace yourself and work at specific points," she said.

After the gun went, Freeman took off. With her opponents spread out between 30 and 42 metres ahead, she couldn't dawdle, there was no time to waste. With only the crowd as company, she pushed hard, digging into the soft grass. A beautifully balanced runner she made it look easy.

She was alone for the first 250 metres and like rabbits, the group of women had bolted out the front.

As she rounded the last bend, with 120 metres to go, Freeman had caught the slowing Deb Tomsett. With the pack of women quickly fatiguing, Cathy pushed again only to contact with a flying elbow from Jackie Chehade as she passed her. Chehade later said Cathy ran into her. Freeman didn't care, and she took aim at Shanie Singleton who was dying out the front.

Passing the cluster of women, Singleton faded as Freeman pushed, urging herself to the line. She breasted the tape, centimetres in front of Singleton in one of the greatest races seen on Australian soil.

For Freeman it's a memory that will stay with her forever.

"There are reasons we have these memories aren't there," she said rhetorically. "Significant moments stay with us. Atlanta is one, of course Sydney is another, but the race at Stawell is another one. I love the place and the people."

"I wanted to win this race. I am a competitor and I have a hatred of losing, it drives me. I just go into such a primal existence that nothing else matters. Obviously, there were days that I lost but there is no thinking really, it's just that nothing else matters, I have to race, I have to run."

As far as the contact with Chehade she didn't really think too much about it. For Chehade, its became infamous, for Freeman she paid it no mind.

"The hit was a surprise but it didn't bother me much. You cant help but take it personally and think well this woman is trying to stop me here. It was like a knee-jerk reaction from her I think but I just had to keep running."

After the race she asked an official what the race time was and they said 54.5 seconds. She was disappointed, it was slow.

In actual fact she had misheard. It was a sizzling 50.45 seconds and a remarkable world-class time, especially on a grass track,

running as a back-marker, dodging all the other competitors.

Converted to perfect conditions on a synthetic track, many think it's a sub 49-seconds run. To put it into context, her time in the gold medal performance in Sydney was 49.11 seconds. Her Stawell run was world class!

Almost as soon as the dust settled on Stawell in 1996, she went straight to the airport and focused on her assault on the Atlanta Olympics three months later and her nemesis Marie Jose Perec.

"There is no doubt the Stawell 400 helped my preparations for Atlanta," she said.

"It is part of the journey. There was something in the back of my mind I think that helped me understand where it fit in the big picture."

Freeman was frank in her assessment of the effect of the race itself. "I shouldn't be surprised that the Stawell Gift, gifted me the opportunity and was a stepping stone to a world stage. It helped me physically and it helped me mentally. I have never been pushed like I was that day at Stawell. It helped me understand my nature and getting back to how competitive I could be and what my body was capable of doing," Freeman recalled.

"In 400 metre running, being able to stay relaxed when you

are so far behind, that takes a kind of a mindset in itself. The fact I didn't freak out or panic or tighten up, are things that help you.

"I have always relished an opportunity to compete, although I could always leave it on the track. If I got beaten it is fair and square. The Stawell Gift of 96 I had to really work hard, I had to earn it. Give respect to the girls and those around who enabled that opportunity."

There is a story going around that she famously wrote "48.60 ATLANTA" in big bold letters on an airsickness bag, as her goal before the event. Incredibly she ran 48.63 but was beaten by Perec who ran an amazing time of 48.25 seconds.

Peter Fortune was Freeman's coach from the age of 18. He oversaw her rise to Olympic glory and, other than a small break for a year or so, they were inseparable.

Not enough has been said of his efforts with Freeman. A quietly spoken man and master coach. He isn't prone to hyperbole either. He's from a different era. An era where actions speak louder than words and the times you run, mean everything.

"I got involved with a superstar and everybody thinks you're fantastic, they think it must be because of you, not the fact the

athlete has got massive talent," he states modestly.

"Cathy is the best female athlete I have ever seen, she was just so dominant. The thing with Cathy was the fact she was talented yes but, she trained so hard. She could get out of shape and into shape quicker than anyone I know."

Her best race has become something of a debate and Fortune felt an Olympic gold medal made all the difference.

"I am happy to debate Cathy because I think her win at the Sydney Olympics was her best run. She doesn't think that. In my opinion you can't beat gold medals. I do love her Stawell win though. It was a tough run and the perfect preparation for the Olympics at Atlanta," Fortune opined.

For Freeman, Sydney is special, because she not only lit the Olympic flame but also because she won the 100th Australian gold medal at an Olympics.

"I don't know what the pressure did to her at the Sydney Olympics, but she seemed to take it in her stride," Fortune said.

"She got the result she wanted and the whole of the country celebrated."

Catherine Freeman was born on the 16th of February 1973 in Mackay, Queensland. Her parents Norman and Cecilia divorced in 1978.

Cathy's mother remarried Bruce Barber. At the age of 10, Bruce told her she would go to the Olympic games one day.

"Both my mother, father and stepdad, had an impact on me in their own way. My stepdad was a jockey and worked with the great horse trainer Tommy Smith. He came from a performance setting in horse racing, and you can imagine it's all about

Australia Post

performance earnings and winnings," she said.

"When he came into my life, he brought those lessons with him. He read a whole heap of self-help books, and he was trying to teach me that thinking differently counts. I read the words I am the world's greatest athlete twice a day, every day. It was repetition."

"Mum was always the one saying don't forget where you come from, think about the Aboriginal and Torres Straight Islander kids and community. Dad was the one who said don't get too big for your boots, you're not too big for a kick up the arse," she laughed.

"Mum is 87 now and lives in Brisbane. She still has a big impact on my life. She's a happy lady and enjoys being a great grandmother. She's one of 13, had five children, ten grandkids and six great grandkids."

Both her father and stepfather have since passed away. Cathy had four siblings and her older sister Anne Marie died in 1990. She had severe cerebral palsy.

"What spurred me on was something far, far different. I was driven by the memory of my sister who had severe cerebral palsy. It was deeply personal for me," she said.

Anne Marie passed away just days after Freeman won her first gold medal at the 1990 Commonwealth Games in Auckland. She spoke frankly about life, family and her indigenous past.

"It always makes me emotional. She passed away in 1990. She was already giving me enough inspiration but when she passed away that became even greater and really fed my determination to forge this path towards being an Olympic champion.

"We grew up in an era where we were ashamed of our blackness. We had a feeling that we were second-class. It's clearly learned behaviour and we observed the trauma in the adults around us. Intergenerational trauma is real, and I am certainly not a victim nor have a victim mindset, but it is real and it affects people," she said.

She referred to the word racism as fear, and as much as she hopes and prays that it will go away, she says it never will.

The conversation flowed and the topic turning to sport and yesteryear. We talked about what used to be shown on television, when we watched not only the Stawell Gift but the likes of boxing, trotting and VFA football.

The Stawell Gift was seen as a big thing in the 60s and 70s and it's said over 20,000 people packed into central park back "in the day". The Stawell Gift isn't what it was, and like boxing, trotting, the Davis Cup and VFA (VFL) football, it's become almost a side bar in the newspaper.

What hasn't changed however, is the love and respect Australia has for Cathy Freeman. Perhaps the most recognisable athlete in Australia.

Freeman transcends time, and in 2026, at the 149th year anniversary of the Stawell Athletic Club, we got a chance to celebrate one of the all-time greats.

2ND Shanie Singleton (Coutts)

"Thirty years on, I can say with complete perspective, that had I won that race, this book may never have been written and that moment may not hold the same place in Australian sporting folklore. I'm genuinely thrilled to have been part of a race that helped bring out a remarkable performance from Cathy. To have pushed one of our greatest athletes in a contest that still resonates three decades later, is something I look back on with pride."

Shanie Singleton (nee Coutts) is the "almost" woman. She almost beat Cathy Freeman. She did have a 30 metre head start though. Not that it mattered. This was pro running and she didn't care. To finish second at Stawell is devastating. In professional athletics, winning is the only thing. There are no silver and bronze medals to hand out.

Shanie, who married 1984 Stawell Gift winner Paul Singleton, was a very good runner. She was a national finalist and at the time had high hopes of making an Australian relay team. She was seasoned, tough, and knew how to run 400 metres.

Her memory is clear of the race finish that day. As the lactic acid burned through her body with a few metres to go, her legs stuck in quicksand, Freeman lifted. Elite runners do that. Singleton thought she had done enough, but a quick glance sideways said otherwise. She had lost by centimetres.

She recalled that Freeman looked much taller hitting the line, simply because she was running so upright and strong. In actual fact, Freeman is three inches shorter.

“I just knew I would have her coming at me,” Singleton recalled.

“My plan was just to try and run her off her legs a little bit and get her to put a good chase on. I knew she was tenacious and she was certainly going to be my main danger in the race.”

When the gun went, Singleton pushed the pace. She had to go early. There was no tactical waiting game today. In a show of pure speed, she quickly caught those in front of her running four wide in the back straight. Once she passed the other women in the race, she had to quickly get back to the line and the shortest way home before they hit the bend. To be left running four wide on the bend was suicide.

Singleton was a class sprinter, no doubt. She looked good and ran with great form with her head held high. Like a scared rabbit she bolted but deep down knew that she was fast using her “petrol tickets”, with payback a hard master. She hoped that it would be enough to stay in front by the time she crossed the line.

400 metres is a race like no other. It’s a tactical sprint. You can’t run a 400 metre sprint race hard for every single metre. Athletes need to find a place to rest or glide, at least for 30 or 40 metres. Knowing when to go hard and when to glide, is a highly specialised art, practised over years of running. Singleton knew she had to throw caution to the wind, in the hope she could surprise Freeman and stay in front.

There was no rest, and it proved to be her undoing.

“I caught the main pack on the back straight but I knew she would be still coming at me” Singleton said of the chasing Freeman.

Behind her, as the runners hit the last bend Freeman was

flying. Like a wave, the crowd noise followed her. The 10,000 strong mob knew they were seeing something special. But could Freeman actually win? Singleton hoped not.

With 100 metres to go, Singleton was still in front but slowing, the electric start was taking a toll.

Freeman was in full flight, and even a stray elbow couldn't halt the Commonwealth Games' Gold medallist. Like the thoroughbred she was, she mowed them down.

Singleton ran the race of her life. It is suggested that she has run the second best 400 metres by a female in Stawell Gift history. It took a once in a lifetime runner to beat her.

She remains upbeat about it and believes if she had won, it would never be remembered.

"Having been beaten by such a legend means it's preserved in history. If I had won it, it would never have been remembered like it is now. It would be just another pro race.

"Her victory went on to mean so much more than just that race – it became part of Australia's sporting story and no doubt inspired young athletes across the country. Cathy herself has spoken of how the win contributed to her belief in herself as an athlete leading into her silver medal performance at the Atlanta Olympic Games later that year," she said.

Singeton is matter of fact about losing, and holds no ill will. "If I had beaten her on that day, that Youtube video wouldn't do what it's done. Good things come from being a loser sometimes. I still get a kick out of it, because she was just an awesome athlete." "It was nice that it meant enough to be in her book." She recognizes what a fantastic run she ran that day.

"I pushed her to a world record grass time and that was

phenomenal. She ran 50.48 on a grass track, being knocked by another runner – it just shows how damn good she was."

Singleton wasn't without great wins over her career. She went on to win the prestigious Devonport 400 metres and won the Wangaratta 400 metres off scratch.

As the the 30th anniversary of one of Australia's best athletic races looms, it wouldn't be unusual for Sharnie to reflect on that time and what was 1996. Time passes quickly and for Singleton she sees the race for what it is, and Cathy Freeman for the champion that she was.

"It's hard to believe it's been 30 years since 'that race'. At the time, I was completely focused on competing, and if I'm honest, on the day I was devastated that I didn't win. As athletes, that's how we're wired – you line up to give your best and you hope that's enough. And it was my best; Cathy was just better – world class better! But, with each year that passed, I came to see the race through a very different lens.

"On reflection, I feel privileged that I was on that grass track at Stawell when Cathy delivered what became one of the most iconic wins in Stawell history.

"Personally, that race, and the sport of both amateur and professional running, gave me something lasting. That day, I knew I had prepared well and run to the best of my ability – I left the track knowing I had given everything, and although I didn't win, it reinforced a lesson sport teaches you – you have to trust your process. That lesson didn't just stay on the track. It shaped the way I approached my career as a teacher and the messages I shared with students. I've always encouraged young people to focus on their preparation, their discipline and their character, rather than just a result. That race highlighted that there are lessons in moments of disappointment and that's something I've tried to pass on to student's I've worked with."

Shanie Singleton raced well into her 30s. The mother of three, lives on the NSW central coast and is a teacher.

1
6
7
Simpli

3RD Tara Gleeson (Gately)

"I believe I was in the right place at the right time that day. And what a privilege and an honour to be part of such an iconic race. It is quite incredible that people who didn't know about my younger days who have seen the race and ask me 'did you run against Cathy Freeman at Stawell? I saw a race and I think that was you.'
That's what is so great about the Professional running scene. We get to run against the best. And to be involved in such a race is just WOW!"

Professional athletics highlights some unusual race distances. Unique to the sport, for example, is the 70 metres; all power and fast moving body parts. It's over in a flash and a blur of colour.

The Gift distance of 120 metres is a time-honoured race that comes from a bizarre beginning. A longer story, the 120 metres is known as the 'Sheffield distance' because it was the gap between two pubs in Sheffield England, and a race that may have taken place between two drunk patrons in the 1800s after an argument as to who was faster.

Tara Gleeson (nee Gately) loved both of those races. It was early in her career and 400 metres scared her. It was long and painful.

The shorter distances suited her better, with her fast twitch muscle fibres exploding like a coiled spring, when the gun went off. She was small in stature but a true "pocket rocket" as the expression goes.

Making the 1996, 400 metre final at Stawell petrified her. She said she lacked confidence in the longer races.

She was nervous going into the final and her expectations were low. A quarter mile is tough going.

"I had mainly considered myself a shorter sprinter and had some success in the lesser distances throughout the year," she recalled.

"The nerves were extremely high and I lacked confidence over the 400m distance. I just didn't want to come last."

Tara had a good plan. Like most of the women in the race she wanted to start hard but find a rhythm and not be silly and go too fast too early.

"My aim in the race was to start hard find a rhythm and hold that for as long as I could, then focus on strong stride coming off the last bend. I had no expectations of placing, except I didn't want to finish last."

Passed by a few runners in the back straight, the pace was on. Concerned that she was running too fast in the early stages, she tried desperately to hang onto the back of the pack.

"I held on to them down the back straight and around the top bend. Coming into the final straight I remember feeling the lactic acid. This was hard.'

She didn't see Cathy, but heard her coming. The crowd told her. Flashing home, she finished a fantastic third and was over the moon.

"I was sitting behind what seemed like a wall of runners in that final straight. Suddenly a gap opened up right in front of me between two of them, I focused on pumping the arms driving the knees. I came through the gap and finished third. At the end, my first words that I remember were along the lines of 'holy crap'. I just finished third at Stawell, and to Cathy Freeman at that.

"I was wrapped, but spent. I'd given it everything and really, the race couldn't have gone any better for me. I surprised myself at how well I ran," she said.

Reflecting on that afternoon, Gleeson thought she was just in the right place at the right time and like most of the women in the race, accepts that she was lucky.

"I believe I was in the right place at the right time that day. And what a privilege and an honour to be part of such an iconic race. That's what is so great about the Professional running scene. We get to run against the best. And to be involved in such a race is just WOW!"

These days, sprinting isn't a priority for Gleeson who admits she misses the camaraderie and the community. She has focused on longer distance events over the past few years including five kilometres, through to full marathons and triathlons.

"I'm still passionate about running. The challenge, the community and striving to get the best out of myself and team mates. The endorphin hit, the sense of achievement, the mental wellbeing and most importantly the people you share the experiences with. I still watch the Stawell Gift every year and I get goosebumps!"

Her first year that she experienced the Stawell Gift was in 1993. She didn't enter any events because she thought she wasn't good enough.

"I thought only fast people run at the Stawell Gift. But when I got there and saw the whole event, I entered every year since. My last race at Stawell was in 2008."

Despite having an affinity with shorter distances, Gleeson

gradually found her feet in the quarter mile and won the Stawell 400 metres in 1999 and again in 2007. These two wins along with her 'Athlete of the Year' Award, are the highlights of a great career in the sport.

"My favourite races would have to be this one (1996 because of Cathy Freeman and the history) and the 1999 and 2007 Stawell wins. The 2007 win is a big one because it was completely unexpected, and more so because it was the last race my mum got to see me run."

"Mum was planning on coming but was too unwell at the time to attend in person, so she watched on TV from the couch at home. It was a highly emotional win because Mum passed away later that year."

Gleeson lives in Melbourne with her husband, and does casual relief teaching work as well as working as a personal trainer. She is also a recreational running coach.

4TH Jackie Chehade (Lewis)

"Directly after the race I may have taken it a bit for granted. Getting older I'm finding I'm doing a lot more reflecting and finding gratitude in the past. I feel very privileged to have been a part of history and to have run in a race with Cathy Freeman who later became an Olympic champion. She's not only a great champion, she's a beautiful person."

South Australian Jackie Chehade (nee Lewis) became famous because of her elbow.

As far as elbows go, I'm sure it was a run of the mill, garden variety type, but her fame came about because it's what she shoved sprint golden girl, Cathy Freeman, in one of the most famous 400 metres races ever seen on Australian soil.

In perhaps Freeman's only ever physical altercation in a race, the clash with Chehade has been replayed over 250,000 times on Youtube. And with good reason!

With no high definition vision available in 1996, the YouTube film is fuzzy, but you can still see the elbow clearly. Freeman is going flat out running wide on the track as they head into the straight.

Whilst flying past fatiguing opponents, what unfolded next had all the drama of a Broadway play, with the ABC television commentator shouting words more akin to an AFL game than a 400 metre race.

Referring to Freeman in the home straight, he hollered, "She goes past Tomsett, she's going to win I think, easily in fact, Lewis gives her a shove."

In a collision more suited to the MCG than an athletics track, Freeman was forced sideways by at least a metre as she clashed with Chehade.

Shaking off the elbow, Freeman recovered her composure and her balance and powered on.

With the commentator riding every Freeman step, he yelled as she crossed the line, "She's done it!"

Chehade ended up running a great race as well and battled on for fourth, unfazed by what happened.

In the eyes of the general public it was a questionable act, but to the professional running community, she was simply holding her ground. It was fair play. Cathy Freeman didn't care. She is made of sterner stuff.

For the 59 year old Chehade, who finished second to Freeman in the same race the year before, it was a curious way to be remembered after all her years in the sport.

"Since social media, our interaction at the top of the straight has been a bit of a topic of conversation," she smiles wryly.

"It seems strange really. I ran for years and this is what I am known for. In actual fact, Cathy moved in on me in that race and I just bumped her off. It's something that happens in all circular races when you are running at speed, there are bumps and hits all the time. If I had my time again I wouldn't do anything different." she said

"I felt an athlete lean into me and I just pushed this person off and kept running. The reason I elbowed was because Cathy leant

into me and I just pushed her off. I was just trying to stand my ground and get into position. Everybody was trying to get into position at the top of the straight to do the best I can."

For Chehade the race seems to get replayed every Easter on social media.

"The elbow part of the story wasn't that well known until Facebook came into the picture. That's when I started seeing the race. Every Easter you see the race on Facebook and the elbow seems to stand out more than anything."

Laughing, Chehade has a feeling the elbow assisted Freeman.

"I think it probably helped Cathy win anyway. I pushed her

onto win and get her into a better position.

"Because there are no lanes in the race you get that quite often. That wasn't the only shove that happened but that was a noticeable one in the straight."

29 years of age in 1996, Chehade was in good form in the lead up. She had won the 800 metres at the Bay Sheffield and the Camden Classic, a respected 400 metre event in South Australia. She went into the 400 final at Stawell with a good race strategy and what she thought, was the right plan to win.

From the gun, she was to start hard and run at almost full pace down the back straight. Around the 200 metre mark the plan was to take a few breaths, glide a bit, and then start to accelerate with 150 metres to go. The general idea was to push off the last bend and with 80 metres to go and give it everything she had.

"I wanted to relax and try and treat it as I would any other race," she recalled.

"All went to plan but much better runners beat me on day. I am satisfied I gave it everything. I gave whatever I had left in the tank and came fourth.

"It was very exciting having a world champion in our race. What a magnificent run by Cathy. You could hear the crowd applauding as she was coming around the oval and got closer to the pack.

"I feel extremely lucky to have been in that race with Cathy and I am privileged to have run for 15 years in the South Australian Athletic league and the Victorian Athletic league."

Chehade came into athletics via boundary umpiring AFL footy back home in Adelaide in 1990. A well worn path into professional running, Chehade was the first female boundary umpire in SANFL history.

She says it was the perfect preseason for a career as a sprinter. Boundary umpiring in the winter and athletics in the summer. "The SANFL was a fabulous preseason for the coming athletics season. I did the Under 17s and reserve grade, but I was the first female in South Australia to do it. Frank McHugh was my coach and he introduced me to pro running."

Chehade has had 30 years to reflect on the 1996 edition of the women's 400 metres at Stawell and like the other women in the race met up with Cathy Freeman over the past few months.

Chehade is married to former Pro runner Amin Chehade. She has two children and lives in Adelaide. She runs her own personal training business.

5TH Emma Yeomans

"To achieve our own goals in life, whether in sports, work, or life in general, we can all learn from her example. The skills she exhibited were applicable not only on the track but in life as well. I like to think that even though I may not have excelled on the athletic field, I still apply many of these skills in my work and studies. Perhaps the lessons I learned in a race that lasted less than a minute, have endured for the past 30 years."

The Sydney Olympics of 2000 was a time of celebration. It had been a big lead up, seven years in fact. Sydney was announced as the games host in September 1993.

A well kept secret, Cathy Freeman had been the surprise packet at the opening ceremony and had lit the flame. It was fitting though, because Freeman ended up being the darling of the Olympics, delivering gold in her pet event, the 400 metres.

Emma Yeomans was 25 weeks pregnant at the Sydney Olympics. Tickets were hard to come by, particular the night of Freemans 400 metre final. Scalpers were selling them for double face value. When extra tickets were released to the public Emma managed to get some for her and her husband, Steve.

Sitting high in the stands, Emma loved it. Being there was all that mattered. For her it was one of the best nights of athletics ever. Tatiana Grigorieva won silver in the Pole Vault and Jai Taurima had qualified for the final in the men's long jump. Mel Gainsford-Taylor, Patrick Johnson, Matt Shirvington, Andrew

Murphy and Mathew Beckenham were all there competing in their respective events. It was a night to remember.

Widely regarded as the best Olympics games ever, Sydney remains a magnificent memory for millions of Australians. Emma Yeomans was no different.

"The crowd was so excited to be there," she recalled. "I was nervous. My poor baby must have received so much nervous energy and adrenaline from me that night."

Freeman wore the now famous Nike body suit, which stretched from her ankles to over her head. Emma and Steve looked at each other wondering if she was going to actually race in it.

Freeman was favourite going into the final. Yeomans and her husband were sitting in the stands at about the 200 metre mark.

"As she cruised down the back straight, I started to panic. She did not look to be going hard enough. In hindsight I think she looked just like she did that day at Stawell, calm, focused and floating over the track. Ninety percent of the crowd must have been cheering her on. As she came into the straight, we knew she had the race won. Nothing was going to stop her. She crossed the line and squatted down and she took in all the emotions. I had tears in my eyes. Everyone was standing and cheering."

Aside from her wedding and the birth of her two boys, Yeomans says it was one of the best days of her life.

For Emma Yeomans running was love at first sight. She started at Little Athletics and her mother says she was addicted to it.

Following little 'As' she started on senior athletics and in 1991 she joined the Victorian athletic League.

"I had grown up watching the Stawell gift on the TV with my Dad. It was so exciting to be there. Running in the handicap events was exhilarating. I loved the sport and the thrill of the chase. When I first started with the VAL, there weren't many 400m races for girls. My first year at Stawell was 1993 and I made the final of the women's 100m."

Plagued by injuries in the lead up to the 1996 Stawell Gift, Yeomans managed to recover enough for a last-ditch effort and she recalls feeling nervous in the lead up to her heat. She wanted to run well and finish what had been a tough season hampered by hamstring injuries. Winning through to the final she knew she faced tough opponents in not only Cathy Freeman but the other females who had run well during the season.

"I remember thinking we didn't really expect Cathy to win. She had to give us such a big start and I knew there were others running well that season. Shanie Singleton was on fire.

There was something about Cathy's presence – she managed to appear calm, inspiring, and formidable all at once, and she was often hard to read."

As the race approached on Easter Monday, like most athletes Yeomans was nervous. Quick trips to the bathroom are always on the agenda for an athlete closing in on race time, which can be problematic when wearing spikes.

"I felt alright and hoped for a strong performance. I knew I had to start aggressively, praying the recent training block would pay off."

If you look at the footage, Yeomans was the first to kick hard. Up and running early in the race, she ran two wide on the first bend. Singleton was pushing from the back.

"Perhaps I pushed a bit too hard, but with Freeman on your heels, there was no room for relaxation. I felt strong as I ran down the back straight, overtaking a few competitors. I vividly remember the transition from feeling good, to the onset of lactic acid though. Suddenly I was spent. It felt like the longest last straight I had ever run.

"The crowd's roar grew louder, signalling Cathy's approach. Her silent, long strides seemed to glide effortlessly across the ground as she surged past us."

"It was truly incredible that she won the race. Initially, she didn't seem excited, but once she heard her time and realised what she had accomplished on grass, going wide around the entire field, she must have been pleased."

"The atmosphere on the track that day was electric. Everyone was there to watch her, and there was a palpable buzz that likely propelled not only her but, all of us, through the race. I feel very privileged to have been part of this historic run. I remember re-watching that race when I got home, and I couldn't believe how relaxed Cathy looked as she ran down the back straight while we were all giving it our best. She gave us such a head start. How did she remain so calm?"

The following year Yeomans was to have her best season. She won nine Victorian Athletic league races over 300 and 400 metre distances and medalled at the state championships.

She had also made the 1997 Stawell 400 metre final.

"Although I do not race anymore, we are still involved in athletics. Steve coaches athletes. Both our boys, Geordie and Toby, have competed in amateurs and VAL. Geordie has won a few races and after a couple of years of injuries is trying to get back to racing. Toby was a gymnast but competed at Stawell in the Little Aths events and was on the program one year.

"Participating in this race has been an incredible experience, not just on the day itself but for many years in my athletics career. The excitement I felt that day not only boosted my confidence in running but also inspired me. It marked a pivotal moment for me, as I believe my dedication to training and competing intensified over the following years until I retired from running.

"Athletics is such an amazing sport to compete in and be part of. The VAL will always have a place in my heart as it was such a great time of my life and I do miss it. I have met some great people who are now friends, and even met my husband through the sport. I have loved reminiscing about my days of racing, and socialising. It has bought back so many great memories.

"I remember some girls being intimidated by Cathy but I relished it. I can proudly say I raced against an Olympian, a world champion, and an Australian legend.

"Witnessing someone as remarkable as Cathy progress to world championships and ultimately win gold in Sydney in 2000 demonstrated her dedication and focus. Observing her achievements at such a young age was truly inspiring. To achieve our own goals in life, whether in sports, work, or life in general, we can all learn from her example."

Emma lives in Melbourne, has two boys and works at the Monash hospital as a clinical trials coordinator.

Kim with her father..

6TH Kim McDonough (Holloway)

"I still feel grateful every year to walk through those gates at Stawell. I take a deep breath and take it all in. That race in 1996, really set me on a path and I have stayed on it ever since. I always reflect on that first final when I step out to warm up on Central Park each year, it's just as special now as it was that day in 1996. I love that race. I loved the way I felt being a part of it, I felt a natural high that I wanted to feel again and again. My dad always said this sport gets in your blood, I caught the bug that day and 30 years later I still haven't left. It's just a way of life now. I feel quite emotional and proud when this race is talked about many years later."

The 1996 400 metre final was Kim McDonough's first final at Stawell. She got through after finishing second to Jackie Chehade in the heat on Saturday. She was the fastest qualifier. Stawell was special. Her father was born there. She grew up playing on the manicured lawns and running around the old grandstand. The Stawell Gift was in her DNA, and Central Park felt like home.

Many come into this sport through family. McDonough was one of those. She followed in her father footsteps and eventually met her husband in the sport.

"Dad won the Dimboola Gift in 1948. I have the sash at home. As a boy dad sold the Stawell programs outside the ground and as kids, we would sit up on the hill and watch the running. Dad would take us around behind the starter to listen to starter's commands," McDonough said.

"My dad was over the moon when I had made the final. For years, a framed photo of the finish with all seven girls in a line coming up the home straight, hung proudly in my parent's house. Dad would show it to everyone who visited. He loved that race and talked about it for years," she says.

At 19 years of age, she was the youngest in the field. Light on her feet and a good technician, she wasn't without a chance but, she was up against race hardened, veteran women, and a once in a generation Australian legend. It was going to be tough.

Now 49 years of age she recalls the race like it was yesterday and it holds a special place in her heart.

"I was pretty raw at the time, but that's the race that is most memorable for me. It was my first Stawell final, and it really wasn't about the win or the sash."

It was cold that Easter Monday. Easter can be like that. At least the rain stayed away, unlike the previous year, when the track was heavy with water.

McDonough was nervous. She watched Cathy warm up next to her. Sizing her up she couldn't help but notice how fit and professional she looked.

"I remember thinking how lucky I was to be out there and I wouldn't want to be anywhere else. When the gun went, my main memory was that it was fast! It was so much faster than any race we had done that season. Race plans went out the window and I forgot to relax. The pace was on and we were all running on adrenaline."

Running in the blue singlet off a mark of 36 metres, McDonough started the race six metres in front of Shanie Singleton. She turned into the back straight running two wide.

As Singleton passed her and they approached the last bend, McDonough, who was running a good race, ended up three wide, working hard to get past other runners.

"It was loud, and they got louder as Cathy got closer. The noise let us know she was coming before we knew she was there. The race was a blur and over before we knew it, She went past in the home straight full of running. I actually didn't know Cathy had won until it was announced officially," she said.

Freeman's time of 50.4 seconds was the fastest by a female at Central Park, ever. Nobody really knows if grass track records are real but if they are, Cathy Freeman's run that day would have been a world record.

"Her run was sensational," McDonough gushes. "It didn't really hit home straight away, actually how good the run was. We all ran fast times because of her, we ran times far above what we could usually run.

"I think we are all proud to have been a small part of a race that was the start of friendships and has become an enduring piece of Stawell and Australian sporting history. We all have our own memories of it. I now feel quite emotional when this race is talked about," she says.

"We all share a bond of being in that final together. Whenever we see someone from that race, we share a hug and talk about it. All of us girls share a bond of being in that final together.

"Seeing Cathy do a lap of honour was a memory I won't forget, something I haven't witnessed before or since, at Stawell. She looked incredibly fit and was in the shape of her life that day.

"Later that year, I set my alarm to get up and watch her win a silver medal at the Olympics, her fastest ever run and it felt like we had all been out on the track to witness the start of that journey at Stawell."

For McDonough its always been more about community than winning. Still an avid runner in the Victorian athletic League, in the 2026 season she won an open women's 400 and is focusing on another good performance at Stawell.

"What a great sport, to be able to travel to different towns to compete and share this with people you love, I treasure these times with my parents, and then later with my husband. The tradition now continues as we share it with our two boys.

"It's the place I have always felt most myself, and most at home. While life carries on with its many ups and downs, it's been the one constant for me over the last 31 years. I love training, and on race day it's the place I can always rely on to see a friendly face. It's the running community that is most special. My memories will be of the people I've met, the lifelong friends I've made. I love the comradeship out on the warm up track and catching up with old and new friends. We walk to the start line together and go into battle together. We experience races together and share in each other's highs and lows."

"I never would have dreamed I'd still be out there having a run. I feel so fortunate that I am. To be able to reunite with the other six incredible women and friends from the 1996 final, and hear their memories of the race and the paths their lives have taken has meant the world."

Kim works with the Victorian Athletic League, lives in Geelong and is the mother of two boys.

7TH Debra Tomsett

"It's one of the best runs I have seen. When she passed me, I hardly felt her at all. She was so quiet, so smooth the way she ran. I did not appreciate this race until 20 years later. It was just a sensational run. The only other time I've ever seen a great run was Debbie Flintoff King winning her 400 metres hurdles (Seoul Olympics) and her dip at the line."

Debra Tomsett was a 15 year veteran of the Stawell Gift by the time the 1996 event rolled around.

At 38 years of age and the mother of two boys, she was the oldest runner in the field. A seasoned athlete, she had won numerous Victorian Athletic League races and, had a handful of state 200 and 400 meter hurdle titles to her name. She had never won at Stawell though.

In 1985 she represented Australia at the Pacific Conference Games in Los Angeles. She missed out on the qualifying time for selection for the summer Olympics in Los Angeles in 1984 by 0.07 of a second for the 400 metre hurdles.

She also made the final of the inaugural women's 100 metres at the Stawell Gift in 1989.

She was a handy runner no doubt, but in 1996, her best was probably behind her.

In 1996 she was in the full swing dealing with life, family, work and a mortgage. Her family camped out with friends at the local caravan park. It was a yearly event and like a lot of people that take the journey up the highway every Easter, the Stawell Gift was a pilgrimage, a rusted-on part of family life.

“By 1996, my husband Mark and I, along with our Doncaster athletic club friends had been going to the Stawell Easter meet for over 15 years and we camped at the local tourist park,” she remembered. “Camping with young boys was a challenge in itself,” she laughed.

She didn’t know she was part of one of Stawell’s most iconic races for about 20 years.

“It wasn’t until the Freeman documentary came out over 20 years later, that I saw a replay of the race. In the 90’s there wasn’t much, if any, access to the internet on your mobile phone, let alone social media.”

“My son Brett received a call from one of his friends asking whether I had run against Cathy Freeman. Someone then sent me a link to the race and I saw it for the first time. It was an incredible race by Cath. It must have been heartbreaking for Sharni at the time, but history shows Cath winning silver in the Atlanta Olympics three months later.”

Now 68 years of age, Tomsett has a clear memory of the day, although not for reasons you might think, she was far too busy keeping track of her boys to worry too much about the running.

“I was turning 39 in 1996 and had two little boys, Brett (6) and Luke (4). I was kept pretty busy and distracted to think too much on the Saturday before the heat, let alone the final on Monday,” she recalled. “The boys were probably playing with other kids on the hill and weren’t really aware of me running at all.”

In 1996 the circular events at Stawell finished in front of the

small grandstand. In a change that's great for television, all circular races now finish in front of the famous old grandstand on the town side of central park.

"To win my heat I had to swing wide to pass the field to sight the finish line. Having the slight uphill to the finish helped me. I was surprised but excited to win my heat and make the final."

Tomsett was the outmarker running in the black colour. She had a 42 metre head start on Freeman.

Once the gun went, the runners behind Tomsett attacked. With a turn of speed it was Emma Yeomans who was the first to pass her. Then it was the fast running Shanie Singleton. By the time they got to the last bend Tomsett was second last, with only Freeman behind her. Her race was run.

"Once the field started to pass me and coming into the final straight, instinct kicked in and I swung wide to sight the finish line, even though most of the field had already passed me. I had to see the finish line," she recalled.

Tomsett finished last in the race and although she knew Freeman must have run well, she didn't know that history had been created. On reflection, she was thankful for the fact Freeman ran so well.

"After the race I was unaware of the enormity of Cath's finish to win the race. I don't recall anyone on the day asking me about the race. I was probably lucky that it was such a stunning race by Cath and thankfully no one asked me where I finished," she laughed.

"I can tell you since then, I have had many people ask me about the race, as my name was mentioned a few times. I very much appreciate being part of the Stawell Gift folklore associated with this race. People are impressed enough with me being in the race."

After meeting Freeman earlier this year Tomsett was surprised how approachable and easy going she was.

"She is one of the most chilled people I have ever met and so approachable. I was so excited and proud that I posted photos of the race on my Facebook along with one of me with Cathy.

"I so believe that it didn't matter where you finished in the race, it made all of us legends."

Debra Tomsett now lives in the Melbourne suburb of Ringwood.

V. T. DEANE
1946
1946 7 yds, $11\frac{14}{16}$ sec.

C. G. HEATH
1933
1933 11 yds, $11\frac{10}{16}$ sec.

Tom Deane/ Cyril "Goldie" Heath

Decades ago, professional athletics was a way of life in Australia. If you could run fast you could earn money. Tom Deane, winner of the 1946 Stawell Gift, the world's richest professional sprint race said, "You can't eat medals."

Deane wasn't keen on the gold, silver and bronze medals awarded to amateur athletes. A medal didn't put food on the table. Lured to athletics by the prizemoney, "Dasher" Deane won the Stawell Gift the first year after the war, when money was harder to get than ever. He died on the 26th of August 2019 at 97 years of age.

Regional football ovals transformed into professional athletic tracks and towns came alive. Lured by exciting races, dramatic finishes and money, crowds packed into race meetings. Betting was big and the sport flourished. On a successful day, if you were fast enough or smart enough, runners and punters could do extremely well. The perfect post war tonic, a Gift meeting was a godsend for a country town in the grip of wartime rationing. In front of more the 25,000 people, Tom Deane became a household name by winning a race that was arguably once as prestigious as the Melbourne Cup.

Uniquely called "pedestrianism", most people recognise professional athletics through the Stawell Gift, the most famous of the professional races. A small country town, Stawell, in the West of Victoria, hosts the world's richest sprint race and has done so since 1878. It is said that the "Gift" distance of 130 yards, or 120 metres, originated in England, being the distance between two local pubs in Sheffield.

To find the nexus of professional athletics in Australia, you need to look back to the turbulent times of the Victorian goldfields. To break the boredom of fossicking for gold seven days a week, men raced each other. With prizes of money, livestock and gold nuggets, the competition was hot. Mostly match races, in a best-of-three competition, the opportunity to have 'a wager' on the outcome was popular.

Known as running "Pro", 1964 Stawell Gift winner Noel Hussey likened it to horseracing.

"Stawell was referred to as the Melbourne Cup of pro running," Hussey said. "It was the same as horse racing. The punting and handicaps make it different to other sports."

In days gone past, names like Arthur Postle, Bill Howard, and Jack Donaldson were the brightest stars of the professional running world. Great professional runners were adored and the Stawell Gift winner was a darling of Australian sport. The comparison to thoroughbred racing is uncanny and rather comically, professional athletes tended to train in groups called "stables". Aside from prizemoney, betting was a priority, and for good reason.

In 1945 the average costs of a home in Australia was 1,700 pounds. At some of the bigger athletics meetings with up to 15 bookmakers in attendance, more than triple that could be won with well placed bets. For Noel Hussey it was the sole reason the game survived.

"It was what made the sport great. A chance to make a few quid at a time when money was scarce, made it very popular. If you were part of a betting plunge you could set yourself up for life", he said. "Pro running is an intriguing game. Its a game of betting and it's a game of cunning."

Early in the twentieth century athletes were supported by "backers", or a manager of sorts. In a type of ownership arrangement, the "backer" provided wages and living expenses. In return, the runner raced.

"When you have prizemoney, punters and bookmakers," Hussey said, "you are always going to have some villains and some very ordinary people around."

Running was seen as a way to get rich. Runners, punters and backers would do anything, legal or illegal. Much like the infamous Fine Cotton affair in thoroughbred racing, champion athletes were passed off as novice runners. "Ring-ins", were not uncommon. There is also the suggestion that athletes lose or "throw" races to improve a handicap. "Running dead" was a well-used expression for athletes searching for a "no lose" handicap mark.

In the drive for glory and riches, doping was also prevalent. A deadly cocktail of arsenic, strychnine and cocaine was used to improve a performance. Stories of professional runners dying at an early age were not uncommon. For Hussey it was part of the sport.

"It was never really spoken about but people did a lot of things to win. There were a lot of underhanded things happen over the years. It's the same as in horse racing," he said.

"People will do almost anything to win. If you get it right and you backed a runner early at good odds, you could make a lot of money. This is the reason the sport was big."

Tom Deane was born in 1922 in Wahring, near Nagambie in country Victoria. As an 18 year old he signed up to fight in the Second World War, first with the Light Horse brigade and then the Armoured division in New Guinea. He says his talent came from his mother, a regular winner of the "married women's races" at sports days. His grandfather, PJ Breen, won the 1894 Stawell Gift. Running was in his blood. Deane ran in local army races, won a lot, but admitted he didn't know what he was doing.
"I was just running for fun. I went ok at it but it was just a good time really," he said.

A natural sportsman, Tom played in two premierships with Tatura in the Goulburn Valley football league. He was good enough to be signed with Geelong but didn't join the Cats, preferring to stay on the farm. There wasn't any money in football in those days. Discharged from the army in 1945, Deane returned to Nagambie in country Victoria and married his sweetheart, Veronica. They eventually had six kids.

Local sporting hero, Cyril "Goldie" Heath, got wind of his return. Heath won the 1933 version of the Stawell Gift. An unknown sprinter that was fleet of foot? For Goldie it was too good to be true. Sniffing a chance to make a few bucks, he approached Deane with an offer to train him. Deane didn't need convincing.

"Nobody had money after the war. You couldn't get refrigeration, cars or building materials. Even food, clothing, butter, and sugar was still rationed in '46. Things were tough. We lived in pretty poor conditions at the time. We didn't live on steak or anything like that. Goldie was a fisherman and we used to eat a lot of catfish," Deane remembered.

Away from prying eyes Deane trained in a secret location in the middle of the Nagambie lake. It was the same small island where Goldie trained before his 1933 win. Like his coach 13 years before, Deane lived like a monk, leaving the island one day a week for church.

"I did the same program Goldie did when he won. I had to do everything he told me to do, so I did. There was no pleasure in it. It was just hard work. It was 1.5 miles due west from the Nagambie main street," Deane said. "Even getting to the island was difficult. We had to row out in a boat. In Summer we had the problem of bloody snakes in the boat! We milked cows on the island and our training track was just a hard piece of dirt. We just got the 130 yards. If you went 150 yards you went into the Goulburn River. You had to pull up really quick," he laughed.

Lightly raced, Deane won both the Benalla Gift and seventy five yard sprint double, two weeks before Stawell. It should have been a warning the bookies heeded. Rumour has it Goldie Heath got 10 to 1 with his largely unseen and unproven runner in the days leading up to Stawell. Heavily backed, the bookies stood to lose more than 3000 pounds if he won. A strained hamstring in the weeks leading up to the race didn't deter him.

Deane won his heat easily on Easter Saturday. The cat was out of the bag. He was red hot and paying even money. Wearing the same shorts and singlet that Goldie wore 13 years before, Deane's form held up in his semi-final, winning through to the final. He remembers it being standing room only on the Easter Monday in 1946.

“The Stawell papers said there was 25,000 people there on the day. It was packed. The entire oval was shoulder to shoulder. It was the first one after the world war. It was big. I was a bit embarrassed actually.”

Getting better with each race, Deane left his best to last. Off a handicap of seven yards and with an ungainly sprinting style, he won the final in a slick time of 11.87 seconds. Great pro runner Eric Cumming finished second and two-time Carlton premiership player Jim Baird was third. The camp took a lot of money out of the bookies’ ring that day. Deane saw little of it. His prizemoney was enough though.

“I was happy. I got my prizemoney and I had to give Goldie his cut,” he said.

“Goldie won a lot of money from the bookies that day. He did a lot better than I did. My job was to run so I just did that. My family got even-money on me.”

The win set him up for life. Deane won enough to put a down payment on a sheep and cattle station and he purchased a second-hand car. A few days after his Stawell win he won the Bendigo Gift and retired from the sport, handicapped out of contention.

In a sport stacked with stories, Cyril ‘Goldie’ Heath’s 1933 Stawell Gift win remains a good yarn. Like Phar Lap being shot at before the 1930 Melbourne Cup, Heath was attacked on the Easter Monday in Stawell. More than a few of the bookies in attendance didn’t want him to win. They stood to lose over 12,000 pounds if he won. Noel Hussey wasn’t around in 1933 but the story is one

CYRIL G. HEATH.
WINNER - STAWELL GIFT, STAWELL SPRINT, BENDIGO GIFT.
EASTER - 1933.

of legend and he told it like he was there.

"Goldie was attacked on the way to the ground on the Easter Sunday," he said. "A guy walked up to Goldie and tried to kick him. Goldie was wearing those flared type trousers of the time and the lad kicking him managed to get him in the flared part of the trousers and not his leg. Once he realised his plan didn't work, he took off but Goldie was in good form, and got him by the Stawell gates."

The story goes that Heath and his entourage were looking to win a fortune from the bookies. Goldie was quoted as saying, "I chased him and caught him and gave him a couple of lefts. Then my father and brother caught up and got into the act. The man didn't fight back, he just took it."

After Goldie's win the drama continued. Some of the bookmakers left without paying up. Months later, Goldie's father, a big strapping Scotsman paid a visit to the bookmakers, rumour having it he got the majority of what was owed.

Whilst Australia shares a common interest with Scotland as a country that has professional sprinting, the sport isn't what it once was. Tom Dean and Goldie Heath were eulogised as hometown heroes, lauded far and wide. Things have changed. The modern interpretation of the sport is far removed from the 1946 version that sustained a way of life. In years past, the sport beamed proudly off the back page of all the papers. It now sees very little space in the broad sheets.

Whilst the Stawell Gift remains a time-honored event, the days of having 25,000 people packed into a small country football oval are long gone. A bookie or two remain faithful to the sport but punting plunges are rare and big wins are few and far between. Prizemoney hasn't grown proportionally and commercial monoliths like AFL, horse racing and soccer are seen as better options for a punt.

With its origins firmly entrenched in our past, professional athletics is not without historical significance. For this reason alone, it must be remembered as one of the most important sports in Australian history.

William Hadlow

"Boxing people are a special breed, denizens of a strange world that few outsiders see and even fewer understand. It's a dark world that takes what's most savage in man and pushes it centre stage against a backdrop of exploitation and pain. But beyond the spectacle of violent confrontation, boxing offers courage and beauty, loyalty and strength..."

The Black Lights - Inside the World of Professional Boxing

Thomas Hauser

Boxing is a sport of contrasts. In any fight, a man can win a million dollars, or be killed.

Most fighters exist somewhere between the two extremes, scrambling for money fighting in small pubs and clubs around the country. It's a painful, unforgiving sport, full of hurt and punishment.

This is Will Hadlow's world. A professional fighter, Hadlow survived on the lower rungs of the sport. His career wasn't paved with money and world title belts. Boxing was his saviour, and strangely enough gave him more than it took.

Fighters from all around Australia converge on a suburban Melbourne sports complex to do battle.

Hadlow is boxing Namibian Johannes Mwetupunga for the Australian middleweight title. Possessing typical boxing features, William Hadlow has a flat nose and a brooding, aggressive face. Pre-fight he walked around the ring with a scowl and punched his gloves together.

As the bell rang to start the fight, so began my admiration of Will Hadlow.

The African towered over him. He had long lean arms and a chiselled body. With gloves held high in front of his face, Hadlow stalked his taller adversary. He didn't consider moving backwards, or sidewards. There was no stopping him and he moved in a straight line bashing at his opponent's body when he got close.

Hadlow needed to get past the constant long range bombs of the African to do any damage. Fighting close to an opponent is called infighting. With the distance measured in inches, it's tough and hard. Hadlow liked it that way. He was comfortable in a brutal fight and this was that type of fight.

Every punch the African threw seemed to land with a thud on the Australians face. Punch after punch glanced off Hadlow's head. Sweat and blood flew through the air. It wasn't pretty. Boxing isn't beautiful but Hadlow was brave and for many watching this night, he was marvellous.

Round after round passed and Will absorbed punishment, losing the fight but gaining admirers. He was flint tough and didn't take a backward step.

William Hadlow lives on the Gold Coast. His home is a "resort" apartment a couple of blocks from the infamous Cavell Avenue. It's seen better days, and like the hostels of St Kilda and Kings Cross, it's home to full time residents. It's quiet and Hadlow likes it.

His single room overlooked a grimy pool. A BBQ on a tiny balcony served as his kitchen and a pint- sized room housed a shower and toilet. It was a hotel room in another life and he was happy with it. It was home.

Posters of human anatomy hung on the walls courtesy of his studies to be a registered nurse. He works nightshift at a local elderly home and studied nursing during the day.

Hadlow's life was busy, he had to be. I didn't know why until later.

He wore a singlet highlighting broad shoulders, a well-built chest and had arms like steel pipes. He is well groomed and his blue eyes have probably seen too much. He laughs a lot, and wears a permanent scowl, courtesy of a cleft pallet. A deformity causing many battles growing up.

Tattoos cover his body. The largest of them, a rose, sat under his chin, it was the size of a dinner plate. Another faded rose, tattooed beside his right eye has seen better days.

"I guess you want to know about the tattoos," he asked, as if to read my mind.

"I was thinking about roses and flowers and things that grow... you put a seed in shit and it can either not grow, or it can grow into a rose," he said. "I grew through that fertiliser and I would like to think that I am still growing."

Society views Hadlow as someone who uses his brain for nothing more than a target, in the world's roughest sport. That would be a mistake.

Born in Innisfail Queensland in 1975, his father died before he was born, and his mother struggled with mental illness. She was a single parent raising two kids.

At 10 years of age Will and his sister were separated and

placed into foster care. As a ward of the state, he bounced from foster home to foster home for the next five years.

His mother ended her life shortly after he was taken from her. Will doesn't care to think or talk about life in care but he did anyway.

"We experienced a lot of pretty ordinary things growing up that children should never see. My mother was quiet promiscuous with her mental illness. I was surrounded by things that I shouldn't have been," he remembers.

He cried as he talked about life after he was taken from his mother.

"A lot of Foster carers want to help you, but it is a pathway paved to hell... two workers in a home of about 100 kids, they can't protect you all the time."

It was Queensland in the 80s. In big foster homes like the ones Will talked about, carers can be overwhelmed and violence commonplace. He spoke; I listened.

"In this one particular home in Redcliff. Some of the older kids were doing stuff to some of the younger kids that they only do in prison."

The words hung heavy in the air. "There was definitely something in me that made sure that none of that happened to me... I was a tough bastard back then. I had to fight."

His fight had started for real. By the time he was 15 years of age, he had been fostered through eight different foster homes, attending eight different schools. With every new school came a new battle.

Will Hadlow didn't live a childhood, he survived it. These days he has a few close friends but perhaps this discussion was cathartic for him. I asked if he had good people around him. He waited a moment, drew a breath and whispered, "Yes, yes I have." I am not sure I believed him.

In his late teens to mid-20s, he slept where he could, made friends playing Rugby League and lived on couches and in halfway houses. He couldn't hold down a job and was constantly having trouble with the police.

"There is one particular person," he said, "who rang Woolworths up and they gave me a job."

He cried again. "You give someone a job and give them an income. Watch how they change when you give someone a chance."

Reflecting on life could have been a dangerous practice for Hadlow. He needed a distraction. Boxing was perfect for him. "The training was phenomenal and it got me out of the drinking cycle and got (sic) me routine."

When he turned professional he was looking for a payday. Boxing was important in more ways than one.

"It was a way of making money for me, it was a living, and it was a livelihood that I knew. I wasn't earning much but I was getting paid for doing something I loved. I got to do what I wanted to do and I got paid for it. It was my job for a long while."

Former trainer Les Wilson remembers Will Hadlow fondly. Wilson says he was as "strong as an ox and a real likeable bloke."

"William was the type of bloke that fought anybody and everybody. He was very fit, strong and dedicated."

Jarred Fletcher, a Retired world title challenger and Commonwealth Games Gold medallist compared him to a bull. "He was tough as nails. He was never a pretty boxer but just had a huge heart, he would keep moving forward... he was a workhorse and he loved boxing," Fletcher said.

Fletcher and Hadlow fought once and remain friends.

Hadlow's professional record of seven wins, 27 losses and five draws is mediocre. At age 35 he won the Queensland state Middleweight title. He fought for the Australian Middleweight title in 2010, losing a close decision.

"I love the fact that people saw me on stage and I could perform something. It was like theatre," Hadlow said.

"It's that fine line between shitting yourself, to a heightened alertness and sensation of where you are. When you feel that, you will just do what you have got to do. It's like mindfulness and being in the moment. That's my meditation," he said.

Hadlow felt respect but he was knocked out a quarter of the times he stepped into the ring. He said boxing didn't love him. This was the reason.

"When I got those wins under my belt I felt proud, that rush, and that feeling, that was everything I wanted in my entire life. I wanted that feeling that I was important."

"I would put too much pressure on myself to get that feeling again, so, my next fight I would choke."

The very thing he was ashamed of was the thing that saved him. Les Wilson summed it up.

"A lot of time he fought a lot bigger guys and got knocked out. When no one else would fight a bloke, William would fight them. He also lost fights he should have won. He was very hard done by."

Will Hadlow was what is known as a boxing journeyman. Highlighting the darker side of the fight game, journeymen are expected to lose heroically. It's a sad truth but results are often skewed to the hometown fighter.

Towards the end of his career losing became a habit and to save him from further punishment, the Queensland Boxing Authority took his license to fight away. Hadlow took aim at the organisation with the same vitriol he reserved for opponents in the ring.

"I was fighting for a living, they took that away from me. I have never had much money and I have never been able to hold down a full-time job, ever. That's one of our basic needs, is security, and they took that from me."

Hadlow's last fight was a loss to Sydneysider Aaron Lai in 2014.

Hadlow knows how vital the sport is. "Boxing played a very important role in my life. It saved me more times than I care to remember," he said.

"I tried to run away from my problems but you only need one thing to hold onto and I used boxing. That was the one thing, no matter if the rest of my life was falling apart around me, I had that one thing".

Now 46 years old, Will continues to work nights and study nursing.

"I eventually want to be a paramedic. It might take me another 50 years but I don't particularly care. The value of education is awesome. I love going to the gym to work out my body and this is like taking my brains to the gym and working out my mind."

"It's good tools to face this world and for me I took in an opportunity to get an education and challenge myself.

"I am pretty happy and life has taken another step up. For me I need challenges and this is another challenge."

He now offers to others what wasn't offered to him.

"I can't believe I am getting paid for doing something I love. The reason I love it is because I get to help vulnerable people feel better about themselves."

"I can't pretty things up for you. I don't want people to listen to this and get depressed."

He now fights for others, his ring the hospitals wards and health centres he works in.

I was going about my business one day and I received a text from Will.

It read. "I appreciate your interest in my story. We all have a journey to travel. I am just glad I didn't let them beat me in the end. My story hasn't defined who I am and it's not over yet. All the best my friend. Proud to have met you."

He also included a photo. It was a Bachelor of Nursing certificate from the Griffith University.

"I work two nights a week at Fairhaven Detox unit run by the Salvation Army. I also work two nights a week at Currumbin clinic a mental wellness hospital."

"Fairhaven is a permanent part time gig, I enjoy working for them the most because they accept all people from all different backgrounds. I feel I have a deep empathy with people suffering from homelessness, addiction, a background of abuse and generational poverty. Believe it or not in a first world nation, people live in poverty."

"Currumbin is a private clinic so the difference between the 'haves and have nots' is obvious. But I believe I treat every person with full respect and dignity.

"I feel I can relate to broken people, I feel I am no different to them."

Will Hadlow may not have been Australia's greatest boxer but he could very well be our best fighter.

Tim Clarke (AFL photos)

David Clarke (AFL photos)

Tim and David Clarke

The Clarke family from Torquay are a talented bunch. With Aussie rules at its heart, David Snr was a Geelong football club legend in 70s and 80s. His two sons were also handy footballers. 45 year old David Jnr played with the Geelong and Carlton football Clubs. 43 year old younger brother Tim, played for the Hawthorn Football Club and the youngest of the siblings, Georgie, represented Australia at the Sydney Olympics in athletics.

Other than football and family, the brothers share an unusual bond. By an odd quirk of fate, separately, and years apart, the Clarke Brothers were confronted by terrorism.

On a Bali holiday, David and the Geelong Football club sat in Paddy's bar in Kuta at the same time every night. For 10 straight nights they did the same thing. The last day of the trip was different though. David and the team were late to the bar. It saved them. Paddy's Bar was blown up in the 2002 Bali bombings. 202 people lost their lives and hundreds more were injured.

Tim ran a great race in the 2013 Boston Marathon. He

had finished and was recovering one street from the finishing line when the ground shook. Two bombs were detonated by terrorists at the finish line. Three people died and another 264 were injured.

The Clarke brothers were as close to terror as anybody and saw things nobody should see. They don't dwell on their experiences but recall every moment as if it was yesterday.

David Clarke was a solid AFL Player. He was selected by Geelong in the 1998 draft as a father/son draft pick and ended up playing 101 games of AFL footy. He is a funny guy and he likes to joke around. He has a welded-on smile and a rugged demeanour.

Unshaven, he looks like he was awake most of the night with one of his four kids. He shakes it off though and we order a coffee.

We met in a café in Moonee Ponds. He works as a policeman and is a football nomad. He finished his AFL career with Carlton and is now involved in suburban junior football in Melbourne.

He speaks openly about the Bali experience. The conversation flows. He felt he wasn't affected by it. Its only when talking about the effects on his friends that he changes. He slows down and becomes very deliberate.

"Some people I played with who are well known and in the media these days are still dealing with the effects of Bali. I think I am ok but others are struggling," he said.

He didn't mention any names and I didn't ask. It didn't seem right.

"A lot of us still stay in contact and whilst we don't talk about it much, but it is an issue for some of the boys."

Back in 2002 the Cats missed the AFL finals on percentage. After a disappointing season the team headed to Bali to let off steam. Kuta was the destination. A mecca for football clubs of all sorts. Attracted to the bright lights, nightclubs and 24 hour parties, it was a chance for players to relax after a tough season. Paddy's Irish Bar was one of the more popular nightspots in Kuta. Lots of Aussies, plenty of beer and for the single guys, a lot of attractive girls.

A short walk from the hotel, the bar was the designated team assembly point each night. The players got to know bar staff, ate, drank and had a good time. The 'Sari Club', another very popular nightclub, was directly across the road. The players didn't have to go far to find a party.

20 years on, Clarke tells the story like it was yesterday. "After dinner we would get ready for the night and head to Paddy's Bar," he remembered

"Back in those days there was really only a few places that you would go to, mainly Paddy's and the Sari Club."

It was October 12th, and the team was running late. "It was the last night before going home and everyone was tired from the week, so we were not rushing to get to Paddy's."

"It just happened to be the anniversary of the death of Paul Chapman's brother. He was upset and we couldn't get him out of the pool as he was pretty smashed from drinking all day". Poolside, talking and drinking, Clarke felt the blast before he heard it. There was no sound initially, only a rush of air that funnelled through the hotel. Moments later the first of two of explosions shook the very earth under his feet. The hotel rocked. Everything was in slow motion. The shocked players stared wide-eyed at each other. Some swore, some panicked, but mostly they stayed in a dumbfounded silence.

"We didn't know what was going on. The rush of air was really weird and it was followed by the two explosions," Clarke recalled.

Staff at the hotel were the first to move. Scurrying around frantically they searched for damage and any guests who may have been injured. Police and ambulance sirens could be heard over the car alarms that pierced the evening air in unison. Noise seemed to be everywhere.

Gathering themselves, the players cautiously walked out to the street. Panic and confusion reigned. The streets started filling with people. Dazed, confused and screaming, some walked aimlessly and others rushed to get away from the perceived threat. Some were injured and soaked in blood whilst others were black with ash. There were others that lay on the ground motionless.

Shop front windows were blown out and razor sharp glass was strewn across the road. Heavy, thick smoke hung low in the air.

Clarke remembers not having any idea what was going on but has a sharp memory of the day. "We walked down the street and started to see people who were injured. They were bleeding or black from smoke. They appeared to be in shock and some couldn't hear what we were saying. It was mayhem," he said.

"People were screaming and there was just panic from people looking for friends, or those who were disorientated from their injuries."

He shuffled his feet as he spoke and looked at the ground. The happy go lucky Clarke changed into a more sombre version. He seemed comfortable to talk about it, but admitted that he "doesn't like to think about".

"I ran into a mate of mine who was injured. Jake had a large hole in his stomach and there was blood all over him. He also had ankle and achillies injuries. He was there on a separate trip with some other mates. Jake was screaming at us to find his brother who he was with at the Sari Club. His brother was ok in the end.

"I remember getting up the end of the street and turning left to where the Sari club was and it was basically already gone, engulfed in flames. There were people trying to go back into the fire to help their friends, but it was too hot and too late. There were cars on fire and bodies and debris everywhere."

A little past 11pm at night on the 12th of October 2002, a suicide bomber entered Paddy's Bar and detonated a bomb strapped to his body. Those not immediately killed or injured, panicked and ran into the street, straight into another explosion from a car parked strategically on the road in front of the Sari Club.

Exactly one month and one day after the 9/11 terror attacks on the USA, 88 Australians perished, and over 200 others were burned or injured. Violent Islamic group, Jemaah Islamiyah claimed responsibility. Now 42 years old Clarke is a detective in the police force. He says he has learnt to live with the tragedy, a legacy of his training he thinks.

For Clarke it's a memory that will live with him. "I will

never forget it, but I don't think I am affected by it. I sort of put it to the side a bit and don't dwell on it to be honest.

"I don't really remember the weeks after and I didn't have any long-term effects from what we saw but I believe some of the other guys I played with really struggled after it and are still dealing with issues."

Whilst the Geelong Football Club didn't lose any players, other sporting clubs weren't so lucky. North Melbourne players Jason McCartney and Mick Martyn were in Paddy's Bar when the bomb went off. Both suffered burns and were lucky to survive. A touring Hong Kong Rugby sevens side lost 11 people that night. Six members of the Coogee Dolphins Rugby Club died, and seven players from the Kingsley Football Club in South Australia perished.

"We should have been in the bar," Clarke remembers. "We were there every other night at that time. What would have happened if the entire Geelong Football team was in Paddy's Bar at the time?" It's a question that thankfully didn't need to be answered.

The Bali bombings remain the single biggest Australian tragedy on foreign soil outside theatres of war, and the effects are still felt to this day.

Tim Clarke was a runner before he was a footballer. He ran cross country for his school and like his sister Georgie, he was a champion school age athlete. As an AFL player he was quick, nimble and hard to catch. He was drafted at pick 33 in the 1999 AFL draft and played 96 games for the Hawthorn Football Club. It was his love of running that eventually saw him line up in the Boston Marathon on April 15th 2013.

For a marathoner, Boston is a bucket list race. It's the oldest annual marathon in the world. In 2013 Clarke was working with Richmond Football Club coaching its VFL affiliate team "Coburg". He had been training for a marathon for 18 months.

Unlike his brother, Tim is lightly built. He is the type that doesn't put weight on. Thin and lithe, it was his speed and elusive play that almost got him to the 100 game mark with Hawthorn.

In a sport where bigger is better, Tim Clarke was an enigma. A father of two, he's made a career out of football and has coached at Richmond, the Gold Coast and Carlton. A keen student of the game, he is a very good teacher.

Articulate and thoughtful, he doesn't waste words and people listen. His memory is sharp when thinking about Boston

"Boston was on a Monday morning due to the Patriots Day Holiday and we played Williamstown in the VFL on the Saturday in Melbourne. I coached on the Saturday, then on Sunday I flew out of Melbourne and arrived in Boston late afternoon on the Sunday night before the race," he remembers.

He recalls the day like it was yesterday. It was the 121st running of the race and just under 27,000 people lined up to take part. The course swarmed with runners, some there to compete, others to simply participate and have fun. It was a sea of bodies. Like a trail of ants, the runners snaked through the Boston streets, and tens of thousands lined the course to applaud and clap the participants. It was the biggest running event Clarke had taken part in.

"It was huge," he said. "There were people everywhere. The start was packed and the sidewalk was 10 people deep particularly at the finish," he remembered.

A jetlagged Clarke ran two hours 32 minutes and was happy. "I had a terrific race in Boston, I originally set out to run as close to 2.30 as I could.

"Turning the last two corners into Boylston Street was the highlight of the event with the road packed full of cheering supporters. I was lucky enough to enter the street with not too many other athletes around me so I could really take in the atmosphere," he recalled.

He met his wife Bec after the race and the two of them sat in a cake shop around the corner from the finish line. As they reflected on the race enjoying coffee and cake, two explosions rang out through the air.

"At first it sounded like something had fallen onto the ground from a crane or construction site and we didn't think much of it," Clarke said.

"Suddenly hundreds of people were running towards us screaming with panic on their faces. That image is something firmly cemented in my mind, I will never forget it."

Like his brother David, he remembers only confusion and panic around him. People were shouting and running. Police and ambulance sirens screamed through the air whilst marked and unmarked police cars flew around the streets.

Crowds fled the finish line and pushed into the streets screaming to escape. Some knew what happened but most didn't and simply ran in confused terror!

"At this stage we didn't know what was happening and your mind starts to race and you look for danger or something coming our way on the ground or in the air," he said.

"People starting shouting as they ran past... people yelled that there was a shooter and then we heard from someone else who said a bomb went off. It was just mayhem."

The Boston Marathon was in its final stages when two homemade devices exploded at the finish line. Three people were killed, and several hundred others were injured. 12 seconds and approximately 100 metres apart, the two blasts were a deliberate act of terrorism.

The bombs exploded as the race time ticked a little over four hours. Over 5000 runners were still on the course. The race was abandoned as police and emergency workers swarmed the finish line. Carnage ensued. Bodies, debris and blood littered the blast area. Confused race goers and bystanders alike wandered the streets. Family members went missing and people cried.

Social media lit up. Photos of human limbs in blood soaked streets started to hit the airwaves. Uncontrolled, photos of the finish line infiltrated news feeds around the world.

At first the authorities didn't know what happened. It took a while before a terrorism task force was set up. Boston was placed into lockdown and the streets were deserted for some time thereafter.

Two Chechen brothers, Tamerlan Tsarnaev and Dzhokhar Tsarnaev, were found to be responsible and the police started a manhunt. Photos were plastered all over the world. Social media went into meltdown and television networks reported it 24 hours a day. The hospitals were overflowing with the injured. Many lost limbs.

In the minutes following the bomb, Clarke's memory is clear

as information dripped through.

"After about five minutes we were able to get some information from someone about what happened, they mentioned that two bombs had gone off at the finish line of the race. We decided to get away from the area and go two blocks in the other direction in case there was going to be any more explosions in the area," he said.

"TV stations now had images of what happened and speculated that more carnage might ensue. What they didn't know was who was responsible and was there potential for more explosions in the area? After an hour or so, we looked to get back to our hotel which was one block from the finish line.

"The police and army had locked down the whole area with no-one getting in and no-one coming out."

Stranded, the Clarkes got a motel and Tim fell fast asleep physically exhausted from the race and the ensuing chaos. News of the bombing filtered to Australia.

"Relatives and friends started to wake up back in Melbourne to the news of the bomb in Boston and knew that Bec and I were in town. The messages of support and concern were overwhelming."

The next day Tim and his wife Bec left the carnage in Boston for the safety of Australia, as previously planned.

These days Tim is an assistant coach at AFL Club Carlton. He doesn't dwell on what happened but felt he needed closure and he reflected on the event.

"I decided to go back to the finish line later in the year early one morning. I felt I needed to go back and see it. A terrific moment of reflection a friend recommended I do.

"How lucky we were that the bombs didn't go off earlier when I was running past, or when Bec and her friends were sitting in the crowd directly opposite where the bombs went off.

"I could have run a bit slower in that race or the bombers might have arrived earlier and I might not be here. It shows you that timing is everything in life and it's almost like a sliding doors moment."

The Clarke brothers don't sensationalise the events, nor do they try to make sense of terrorism. Who can? They wish it didn't happen of course. but remain optimistic. For Tim it's a focus on the positive that helps.

"David should have been in Paddy's Bar at the time the bomb went off in Bali but he wasn't. Everything is about timing, that's life I guess, and you see it everywhere, in every walk of life. Dave and I are lucky to be here yes, and it could have been so much worse, but it wasn't."

A candid David Clarke looks to the future and he is frank in his assessment of the Bali Bombings. "I think at the end of the day it wasn't our time to go and multiple events occurred that resulted in us not being there at that time. Pure luck really. I have thought about what life would have been like if we lost someone or what my family's life would have been like if I died there. I am also a big believer that you don't stop or restrict the things you want to do in life due to the fear that something may happen."

Ironically, it's worth noting that David and Tims father, David Clarke senior was caught up in a bomb blast in Melbourne in 1986. Constable Angela Taylor was killed when a bomb went off at the city watchhouse in Russell Street on the 27th of March 1986. A story for another day, Clarke Snr huddled in a Russell St Café after the blast and lived to tell the tale.

The Clarke Brothers story isn't a personal tragedy, nor is it a tale of long term post-traumatic stress. What it is though, is a reminder of the continued threat of terrorism across the world and that no one is immune to it.

This is a tale of two footballing brothers, like thousands of footballing brothers around Australia, that came close to death. Terrorism in various forms will continue unabated and unfortunately there will be more incidents and more victims. Hopefully the Clark brothers have avoided falling victim to it.

Ross Knight

Aussie punk band *The Cosmic Psychos* refer to pubs and drinking beer in almost every song they sing. Politically incorrect and loaded with foul language, their tunes are bizarre, quirky and rarely make sense.

On stage or off, it's always 'beer o'clock' and its farmer-come-weightlifter frontman, Ross Knight, that leads the group astray. Knight balances the haywire alcohol fuelled life of a rock star with the dedication of a sports professional. He is a world champion weightlifter. How he does it is anyone's guess.
A contradiction, he burns the candle at both ends. He doesn't care though, he's just having fun.

Ross Knight's farm is called Spring Plains. It's hidden amongst rolling hills near Kyneton in central Victoria. It's been in his family for generations.

There is very little in the way of street signs and you need a map to find it. A rusted gate signals the entry to the property but there is no house in sight. A long dirt driveway awaits me and I remember Knights instructions to close the gate behind me.

Other than the cawing of a crow and a few screeching cockies, its dead quiet. It's beautiful here.

The driveway is long and muddy. The last three days of rain have turned the track into a mud pit. Navigating the waterlogged potholes was problematic and my car was soon caked in mud. The sheep stared at me stupidly and reminded me of why I had to close the gate.

After a 10 minute drive, I arrived at the farm house and was met by a beaming Knight. He was dressed in denim jeans, a flannelette shirt and a frayed baseball cap that had seen better days. He looked every bit the farmer.

He had spent the day working on his bulldozer. Earth moving is his main earner these days. He also grows grapes and produces wine. His long sleeve shirt hides a left arm full of tattoos. He looks strong. Years of farming, sport and weight training have honed his body.

He smiles and shakes my hand. His grip is strong. We launch into some banter about the Kyneton football club that play in the local Bendigo Football League. Like Knight, I played in that league many moons ago. He jokes a lot and pokes fun at himself. I can see why people like him. He likes a laugh and yarn as much as he likes a beer and spends a lot of time doing all three.

The house is surrounded by sheds full of farm equipment and bulldozers. A small silver shed, the type you buy at Bunnings, sits apart from the others. It is the centre of Knights world.

Inside the shed a potbelly stove holds centre stage, along with a few motorbikes. Knight has obvious passions. Motorbikes are just one. He has owned 32 bikes since he was 16 years old.

A radio sits close to the heater. He loves to listen to the footy.

He is a rusted-on Richmond supporter and an ABC radio fan.

Scattered around the shed are weights, barbells, dumbbells, and all manner of lifting gear. For a home gym, its hard core. Knight is a serious weightlifter though. A world champion. His trophies are well hidden. He doesn't want to show me them. "Who cares," he says, shrugging his shoulders.

Like colliding worlds, the shed is also home to Knight's alter ego. The walls are plastered with band paraphernalia, tour T-shirts and beer posters. He is the lead singer of the punk rock band The Cosmic Psychos and it's his recording studio.

Now sixty four years of age, he limps around the farm. He just had both hips replaced, the result of football, running and lifting he thinks.

"I played footy until I was forty-two years old. I have been lifting weights and running for a long time. I had a bit of the farmer strength and I just got into the weights because I thought it might help my footy, which it really didn't," he chuckled.

He calls himself a bad Aussie Rules reserves player and he cuts straight to the point when joking about his sporting career.

"You could say my footy career was long, robust and very below average. I was a great trainer but when I played, I seemed to be everywhere the ball wasn't. My cricket was much the same."

He discovered weightlifting, in an inflight magazine. It looked easy enough he thought. "It had only three exercises so it was perfect for me."

Bendigo was only forty minutes' drive away and had a large weightlifting fraternity. He thought he would give it a go. They welcomed him with open arms.

"I stumbled into this shed full of really good blokes. We were

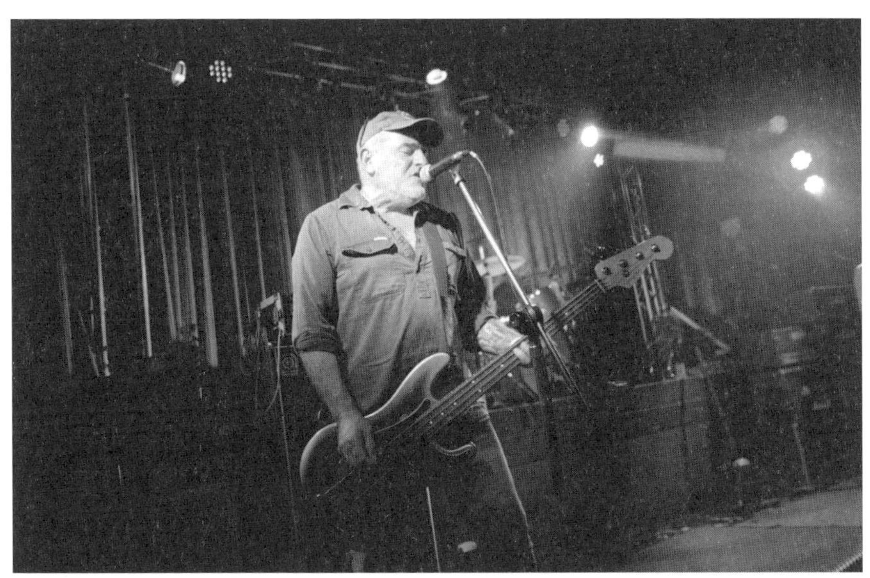

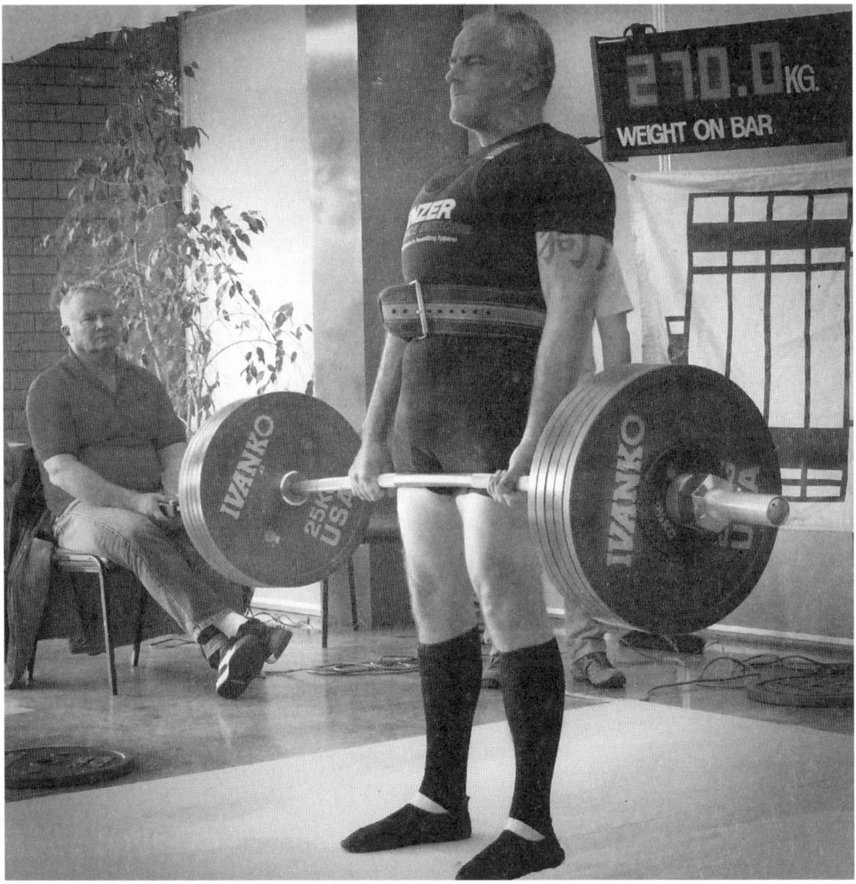
270.0 KG.
WEIGHT ON BAR
IVANKO
25KG
USA
IVANKO

all miss-fits that were keen and dedicated. There were people lifting weights with anger management problems, drinking problems, older guys that had been diagnosed with cancer, people of all ages. They were all there in the brotherhood of lifting heavy and it was perfect for me," he remembers.

When asked about his powerlifting achievements, and with no hint of false modesty, he turned it into a gag.

"The secret to being successful in sport is to pick an obscure one. Design yourself into a weight class where's there's not many competitors and make sure that there is a competition on the other side of the world," he said.

"You lift and you become a world champion. Just don't tell anybody that nobody else actually went."

His smile widened and let out a hearty laugh. Comedy aside, Knight won his age group powerlifting world title in St Petersburg (2003) and Atlanta (2004). Victorian state records and national age group titles support the fact he was a very good lifter.

He struggles with his body these days. With the hip issues and a recurring back problem, heavy lifting might be a distant memory. He's not worried though, he just likes it because it's stress relief.

"Some people like getting shoved in boxes and having their balls tied in knots, me, I lift weights and run just to let off steam." I didn't have a clue what he meant. I still don't.

Married to Karyn, Knight had two sons, Gage and Jika from a previous partner. Jika had quadriplegic cerebral palsy. Wheelchair bound, he can't speak and he has lost his sight. Knight softens when discussing his eldest son.

"You have to be an expert of UFC, wrestling, boxing, acting and nutball. You have to be tough in all the right places to pick him up and handle him," he says with a laugh.

Beneath the jokes there is an affection for his son that drives him. "It's a beautiful father/son relationship. I love him, I miss him when he is not beside me."

The love for his son wasn't lost on me and his motivation was inspiring.

Whilst I was with Knight, Jika returned to the farm with his carer. His wheelchair is one of the big heavy types. Jika sat in the chair overcome by involuntary jerky movements. He recognised his dad's voice. He smiled. Knight touched his arm and with a big smile asked how his afternoon was. This was special.

Knight liked to talk about his son. He was proud of him. "We were told that Jika wouldn't live to be eight years old," he recalled. "My way of getting over that was to stay strong enough to lift him. What he can't do, I will do for him. Well he is 21 now and he is still doing great."

The shed has become a special place for the pair. It's time together.

"I would be grunting and groaning doing the weights and he would start grunting and groaning. He is a funny bugger because when I started struggling, he started laughing," Knight said.

"He can never walk or run and he can never lift a weight. I can do it for him though. That's what drove me to continue lifting weights."

The Cosmic Psychos could be the least well-known famous band in Australian music history. Described as trashy, agricultural, and with a somewhat fuzzy sound, the band has endured four decades. Knight started playing at fifteen years of age with a couple of mates from Kyneton High. He taught himself how to play a guitar with only one string. He concedes he hasn't improved much and only knows how to play two strings now. It seems to be a running joke that his only real talent is in having a laugh.

"Have a look at me as a musician," he says. "I'm an imposter but I have fun. If you can't laugh at yourself, then you can't have a laugh, full stop."

The Eighties was a time when the Melbourne live music scene was on fire. *The Age* Gig Guide was three pages long and according to Knight, "You could pick up a plastic bucket, call yourself a musician and you would get a gig.

"We got a residency at the Tote pub in Collingwood. Every Thursday for a month we would play. Our biggest crowd was seven people."

He chuckled when telling the story. "They felt sorry for us and ended up giving us jugs of beer for free, so it was ok."

His style is unorthodox and a lot of his music was conceived on the bulldozer with the resulting albums recorded in the shed whilst drunk.

With songs like, *Nice day to go to the pub*, *100 Cans of Beer*, *Pub*, and *Your shout*, the Psychos built up a hard core following of pub dwellers and bar flies.

Word of mouth got them a few gigs overseas and Knight still doesn't have a clue how it happened.

He constantly takes the mickey out of himself and his music career wasn't immune to the banter.

"We used to make enough to survive. Our attitude was that

if we spent three months in Europe with all the grog, food and accommodation paid for, then we have had a great time and it was worth it. It was never about money. It can't have been, because we never made any," he said.

Supporting the likes of Nirvana, Pearl Jam and the Mud Honey's, Knight shakes his head remembering a time with the greats of world music.

"We just hung out with these bands in the early days. We were in Seattle when all this grunge stuff happened, and they basically just gave us a mention. I don't know whether it's the music or the fact we just good drinking buddies. It's all just about friendships and being mates."

The Cosmic Phsychos are the good time guys of the Aussie music industry. They have a mate in every town they visit. A good friend of Knights is Pearl Jam frontman, Eddie Vedder.

Knight talks about Vedder like he would a bloke from the footy club. He's like that. Down to earth, he doesn't care much for fame.

"We got to support Pearl Jam when they toured Australia. Ed is a good bloke. He has been to the farm and we catch up when he tours, or when I'm in the US."

Vedder has been quoted as saying some the best nights of his life were spent with the Psychos lead singer.

Knight recalled a funny story. "We went out one night with an actor mate of Eds. We were drinking all night in this kitchen and I was talking to this bloke. We were all shitfaced and I didn't have a clue who this bloke was. I ended up giving him a bit of acting advice. How the hell I knew what I was talking about was anybody's guess."

Knight laughs, slaps his thigh and broke into his signature grin. With a roll of his eyes he announced that the person he was drinking with was actor Bradley Cooper.

Cooper was hanging out with Vedder because he was writing the screenplay for *A Star is Born*. The irony wasn't lost on Knight, "How does a bloody farmer from Kyneton end up hanging out with these types of blokes."

Dean Muller and John "Macka" McKeering made up the Cosmic Psychos trio for many years. Muller has since left the band and there have been others along the journey. A nineteen year veteran of the band, McKeering was once a fan.

"Ross and I met in 1991. I was actually at a gig watching them play. I liked the group and thought they were weird and interesting," he remembered.

Guitarist McKeering rides shotgun to the popularity of Knight and it doesn't worry him at all.

"The bands contribution to Australian music is seen in their attitude and spirit which centres directly around Ross. He is strong and determined and is the best at most things he does. Good bands have a great bass player and Ross is a very good bass player."

McKeering adds, "The reason the band has stood the test of time is because Ross is the best bloke, it's that simple. I'm really lucky that I get to be part of it. Its great fun."

Knight says that if he won Tattslotto, he would record an album every month, and pay Macka a million dollar.

"No one takes the lead and it just works. We can't look at each other without laughing, we're good mates," Knight said.

On the back of a tough 41-gig schedule, Knight is working on a new world tour schedule, which will see him and the brand spend two months in Europe and a month in the United States promoting his last album, called *I Really Like Beer*.

Knight can't remember how many albums they have made but he guessed it was about a dozen. He doesn't like to look back, "because all the albums sound the same anyway."

An enigma, he laughs and jokes about everything he does. He takes a stand against anything serious and he is the secret to the success of the Cosmic Psychos. He won't agree of course.

"I will do this until I stop breathing. I never get nervous on stage. I know I am no bloody good anyway, so it doesn't matter. We have been cool and then uncool. Every 10 years we have a little resurgence and then we disappear off the planet.

"It's all about the fun. I don't do it for the ego, everything I do is about fun. People do things for different reasons. I have never felt comfortable winning all those stupid trophies. I don't mean any disrespect for those people that strive for those trophies, but I don't really care.

"If the farm goes and Karyn runs off with the psychiatrist and my kids end up hating my guts, I could just bum around Europe. It's not about money for me, it's about fun and living life and I am doing that."

Ross Knight is hard at work planning the world tour. Whilst there will be no weight in sight, it goes without saying that there will be plenty of fun, in addition to just a few beers.

Note: Jika has since passed away. He was 26 years of age. Jika was an organ donor and he has contributed to the lives of four other people.

Max Bailey (AFL photos)

Max Bailey

"I remember sitting there as long as possible. I thought it was the last time I was going to be on the MCG. I just sat there for maybe 10 seconds just trying to take it in. I knew I had done the knee straight away. It wasn't as painful as the first one but I knew what I'd done. I remember walking off the ground that day, thinking that was it, I was all done. Not because I didn't want to go again but because I just didn't think they would take a risk on a bloke who had three knee reconstructions."

MAX BAILEY, HAWTHORN PREMIERSHIP PLAYER

The Hawthorn football club won the 2013 AFL Grand Final by defeating the Fremantle Dockers by 15 points. It was a good game but closer than most thought after a dominant season by the Hawks.

An AFL premiership has a habit of producing good yarns. Hawk's skipper Sam Mitchell said ruckman Max Bailey was the pick of them that year. No one would argue, except Max himself. He doesn't like the fanfare. Mitchell was spot on though.

Bailey is warm hearted and modest. Easy to like, the 206 centimetre giant smiles a lot and has a disarming way about him. Talking to him is like chatting to a long lost friend.

He remembers the premiership like it was yesterday. He says the joy will never leave him. Premierships have a habit of doing that. His face lights up when he talks about it. Some players play an entire career and don't get to play in a finals series let alone win a grand final.

The smile disappears quickly when he remembers the other side of the win though. The hospitals, pain, rehabilitation, and the mind-numbing boredom that came with three knee reconstructions. His premiership medal was hard earned, a fitting reward for years of toil.

Cruelled by injuries, Bailey played only 43 of a possible 174 games across eight AFL seasons. Short changed, his life has been full of comebacks.

Born 1986, Bailey hails from Narembeen in Western Australia. It was a small country town about 300 kms from Perth. With a population of just over 400 people, its was typical farming country. The Sun scorched land was worked by flint tough country folk. Sheep and wheat country, there is nothing soft about Narrabeen.

Bailey's home was typical of most in the area. His mother worked the household and his father ran the farm. Bailey played sport and he did chores. He reflected on life back on the farm and the topic quickly turned to his father.

"I remember the day like it was yesterday," he recalled. His words were blunt. He was 10 years old when tragedy struck. "I woke up in the morning and could hear a lot of people in the kitchen. I went out to get breakfast. Mum's whole family were in the house," he recalled.

Baileys words hung in the air. He breathed deeply before continuing to speak. "It turned out my dad had been in a car crash the night before. He was driving home from the pub, just on a country gravel road." He paused before speaking. "Dad hit a tree and that was it."

Baileys father was killed after crashing into a tree. He doesn't remember his father much. It was a long time ago. In his own way, he slices the positive out of it.

"It's strange but without that happening I don't think I would be here right now, I'd still be on the farm. It seems a morbid way of thinking about it, but things are meant to happen."

After his father's death his family moved to Perth. He played football with West Perth in the powerful Western Australian Football League. He was tall, agile and possessed good football skills. It wasn't long before he attracted the attention of AFL talent scouts. He would be a project player. He was raw boned and needed some work. Any club would be looking at his future potential rather than expecting him to play senior football immediately.

Things moved quickly and he was selected by Hawthorn at pick 18 in the 2005 draft. Surprisingly he played his first senior game in round 18 of the 2006 season. It was in the pre-season of 2007, one week after the players returned from the Christmas break when his injury woes started.

Looking forward to staking a claim as a regular senior player, he was struck down with the first of what was three knee injuries. His right knee collapsed twice and his left knee once. Requiring full reconstructions each time, his life became a barrage of surgeries, recoveries, physiotherapy, and medical reviews.

Across his eight year career, he missed close to six seasons of games. Days turned into weeks, weeks morphed into months. He measured his injuries by the season.

In a football club nobody wants to be injured. Almost an outcast, a hurt player leads a lonely life. Bailey's frustration was still apparent years after his last knee reconstruction.

"It was a tough time," he recalled. "You are training at a footy club where the goal is to win premierships, to win games and you can't be a part of that. You've got 50 guys all trying to get themselves up each week. They are coming off injury, they have personal lives and they are looking after themselves.

With little else to do but watch teammates play each week, the frustration of being injured grew.

"Watching your mates play the game you love, watching them celebrate victory and commiserate in defeat, you are unable to do anything but play a waiting game."

Former Hawthorn and Carton Fitness boss, Andrew Russell, provided an insight into an AFL players life.

"I don't think a lot of people realise that to be an elite athlete and especially an elite performer who has come back from such significant injuries, it is just very boring," he said.

"People think AFL footy is exciting. Game day is exciting but behind the scenes it's boring, it's repetitious. It's eating the right things, it's getting enough sleep, it's getting enough rest and it's getting enough time to prepare physically and mentally for the next session."

Russell indicated that the muscle loss after a knee reconstruction could be as much as seven percent in a single day. "It might take a month to get that one day back. So even after two years they might not have the same muscle mass as before the injury. Max got back to doing some ball skills after seven or eight months. To get them going early is just so important."

The red scarring across Baileys knees was obvious, what was harder for others to identify was the deeper psychological bruising. He recalled some dark times.

"There were days where I woke up and I didn't want to go to

training, so I called in sick. I wasn't sick but I couldn't face going into the club, it was the last place I wanted to be," Bailey said.

Bailey simply didn't want to talk about his knee. He didn't want to have the constant conversations about how his knee was improving, or when will he be back to playing or how he was feeling. His knee was improving slowly, too slowly for his liking.

"I just felt really shit about myself. The fact you've got these ups and downs and you are kind of withdrawn and by yourself. Whether or not it was depression I don't know, but it was my idea of what depression was.

"I didn't want to be a whinger though. I didn't want to be the bloke who moped around and felt sorry for himself. The other thing I guess is I am a Christian and I believe in God. I don't know if it is inspiration, but I just felt that I had someone else in my corner. The NZ rugby union player Sonny Bill Williams said something along the lines that whenever everything else was going crap in his life, this (religion) gave him a reason to keep moving forward. I felt a bit like that."

AFL players are measured, analysed, and scrutinized. Kicks, handballs, tackles, marks and a dozen other KPI's are part of a life for players. As a big man Bailey was agile and energetic, a difficult match up for apposition ruckman. Nobody had an easy day playing on Max Bailey, but if you base an opinion of him on data alone, he wasn't in the top bracket of ruckman in the league.

Whilst his career average of nine disposals and 20 hit outs per game isn't elite, his worth was determined by something intangible. Uncomfortable talking about himself, it made what others say about him important.

Not known for his compassion, Hawthorn team of the

century coach, Alistair Clarkson possessed an uncommon empathy for Bailey.

"We wanted to support him for as long as we could. This guy for all his hard work and his commitment to our footy club, has actually suffered these injuries whilst he has worn our colours," Clarkson explained.

The AFL industry is a brutal one. Injury prone players have a limited life span. Knee injuries are particularly bad, a curse for both player and club. A huge investment and a risk, it's not uncommon for athletes to be released from a contract because of injury.

Sacking Bailey wasn't an option for Clarkson. "It would be easier to maybe go our separate ways if he wasn't a great character. We ear marked him from a very early stage when we drafted him that he was a fantastic person first and foremost, a real leader of his peers."

The Hawks had only lost one game up to round 14 of the 2013 season and were early premiership favourites. In the last half of the year, Bailey's twice reconstructed right knee, devoid of cartilage, was proving to be a major concern.

"I knew my knees weren't in great shape, but I had got through the pre-season and it was all looking good until Round 13 or 14," Bailey says.

Alistair Clarkson devised a secret strategy to get him through to the grand final, his pre-planned last game. Bailey didn't tell anyone. A well-kept secret, win lose or draw, Hawthorn's last game of the 2013 season was to be his last.

Whilst he was rested in key games and nursed to the grand final, Bailey played a key role in the decider. His job was to create a contest with giant Fremantle ruckman Aaron Sandilands and allow the other Hawks ruckman David Hale to push forward. Sandilands was the AFL's best ruckman, almost unbeatable but he couldn't be in two positions at once.

"I didn't have the best game but I was thrilled to be out there and for everything to go the way that it did was pretty amazing. I didn't ever dream that I could play AFL football let alone win a premiership. I am so blessed with what happened. I can't really believe it and I don't think I will ever believe it."

Just short of his 27th birthday, he retired from AFL football. He took up a position as development coach at the Richmond football club and following a two-year stint at the Tigers and a Bachelor of business degree, he travelled overseas. In a left of centre move, he worked with The Future Warriors Project, a charity focused on developing men in the local African community. He moved to Tanzania for 12 months.

On his return to Australia, he reflected on his position as coach of Hawthorn affiliate Box Hill in the VFL, being married to Rachel and being a father to Georgia (6), Anna (turning 5), Lucy (turning 3).

"Life has changed for me that's for sure. I love being a dad and I love being married. Life seems really good."

On the cusp of his second year in charge of Box Hill, Covid 19 struck. AFL assistant coaches and VFL coaches across the league found themselves unemployed. Bailey was out of work.

"It might sound stupid, I just believe that was the way it was meant to go and there is something at the end of this," he said. After two years working in the Human resources department of hardware giant Bunnings, Bailey drifted back into the AFL and is now settled back at the Hawks as GM Football Operations.

He remains upbeat. With the loss of his father, three knee reconstructions and a global pandemic to deal with, he has every reason to feel hardly done by. He doesn't.

"I learned that my priorities needed to shift; the order for me right now is faith, family, and then work, whereas work (football) had been number one on that list for a long time and maybe that was necessary but I don't know if it's the way it should be," he said.

Just like the 10-year-old boy back on the farm, he got on with it. For him there was no other way.

"I don't know where I will end up. I have family to think about now but what I do know is that I want to help people as much as I can. I have learnt that about myself. I am pretty bloody blessed to have done the things I have done. The things I have been through, ideally it wouldn't have happened. But if they hadn't, I wouldn't be where I am now.

"It sounds funny now that I am back in the AFL doesn't it! I didn't question the time I had spent in the AFL, moreso that I was questioning whether I should go back into that environment given what I learned during my time away from the game.

"I'm a slow learner, but I did learn to slow down. I learned that not everything is about competition and performance, and that if I got something wrong, I wasn't going to get called out in front of a bunch of teammates or lose my spot because of it."

Susie Ramadan

Women are breaking the shackles in Australian professional sport. With AFLW, The Aussie soccer team The Matildas and women's cricket leading the way, female sportspeople are doing things they haven't done before in Aussie sports.
Boxer Susie Ramadan has been doing things her way well before it became fashionable. With five world titles in three weight divisions to her credit, she has been one of Australia's best fighters, male or female.

Her path to the top was unorthodox. As a Muslim woman, boxing was forbidden. Making a living from her chosen sport has been almost impossible and travelling to far-flung destinations to be world champion hasn't been without its issues.

For Susie the clock is ticking. Father time is harsh in boxing, it sneaks up when you least expect it and smacks you in the mouth.

It's Fight Night in Melbourne. The temperature nudges 30 degrees. The humidity sits heavy in the air. Even the spectators are sweating tonight. The conditions are energy sapping and choking, perhaps the worst type of night for a fighter.

In the dressing rooms it's even hotter. Fighters, trainers, and backslappers pack into the tiny space. It stinks of body odour. Boxers wait their turn to fight, stretching and warming up. Everybody is sweating and moving around. Everyone except Susie

Ramadan. She sits quietly in the corner. She is a professional fighter. She stares absently and waits her turn. She hasn't started warming up but beads of sweat form on her forehead. It's that type of night.

Shunning makeup, Ramadan wears boxing shorts, a bra top, and neatly tied boxing shoes. Standing only one hundred and sixty centimetres tall, she appears fragile. Her shoulders and arms are toned and her hair is pulled back tightly into a plait. Her left leg jitters up and down. It's the only sign she is nervous. She stares at the commotion around her.

Her trainer lingers. Not a word is spoken. He looks at his watch and gives her a nod. It's time. She starts to stretch and jogs on the spot. She doesn't talk but wears a permanent smile. She loves this.

Susie is the only female in the room. She pays it no mind. I glance around searching for the female bathroom. There isn't one. Outside, the crowd look on. Drinking beer and talking, they wait for the carnage to begin.

I met Susie in 2009 as a fresh-faced thirty-year old. A whirling dervish of a fighter, she was a non-stop punching machine. Racking up ten straight victories without a loss, she had the boxing world at her feet. She loved to fight and wanted to be world champion. It was all in front of her.

Move the clock forward to 2026 and she is a hardened veteran of thirty four fights and a five time world champion. She has won and lost the International Boxing Federation Bantamweight title and World Boxing Council Bantamweight title. She also challenged for the IBF Super bantamweight title in 2024 but lost

SYSTRONIC
WBC
SUSIE RAMADAN

to fellow aussie Cherneka Johnson.

With only four defeats in her career, she has struggled to find opponents. The forty three year old is frustrated. Her career had stalled.

"I love the sport," she said, "but the people ruin it. I'm a little bit saddened to be honest."

With only nine fights in 10 years, her biological fight clock is ticking. Age is a disease with no cure in the fight game.

"It's been difficult to get quality fights," she explains. "There aren't enough fighters in this country. In boxing, the window is small, and you have to use it. I need to keep fighting."

She is appears cynical, worn down by the fight game and she wouldn't be the first. It's a tough sport.

"I don't want to fight boxers who can't fight, just so I can get a fight. I won't get better that way. I was asked to change my name in order to get further in my career but I declined," she said, as if to indicate her name had something to do with her not getting fights.

Boxing is a small industry in Australia but for Ramadan being female made it even tougher.

"Being a woman, means it's been hard to get fights. Being a woman in this sport is not only hard to get fights but the fact is, its also a male dominated industry which makes many things difficult, even to be taken seriously," she said.

"The reality is unless you are one of the big names in this country you don't make any money."

A three-round fighter can be paid as little as a thousand dollars per bout. With three months of training, it's a tough way to make a living. Most don't fight full-time. Susie fights because she is good at it and she loves it. At times she gets frustrated but she says she has a thick skin and the challenges push her to work harder.

Born Sunduz Ramadan in the western suburbs of Melbourne, she carries the ring name of Susie Q. A moniker she took after undefeated heavyweight Rocky Marciano's famous right hand punch. Ramadan is Australia's first female Muslim professional boxer. She has been condemned and criticized by Islamic elders. Boxing violates the Muslim belief of modesty. Fighters are barely clothed, of course.

"I am a girl so I expect to be criticised," she said. "I am also Muslim, which is something very different. As far as boxing and the sport itself, it's not encouraged due to striking someone in the face. It goes against our religion."

She has the Quran saved on her iPod. Listening to it regularly, it helps her navigate the cut throat world of professional boxing.

"God gave me world titles to use for good. He gave me the talent to use. It's in his hands. I feel that people look at me and get inspired. Isn't that a good thing?" she asked rhetorically. "It's important to me. But more in the way of having a focus and a goal. It's like meditation."

The religious period of Ramadan is an important month for Muslims. A month of fasting from sun up to sun down, hasn't been without its challenges.

"I try my best to observe Ramadan but with training and fighting it's almost impossible to fast during the day. It's probably not good for my health but I do try. I need to be flexible."

Not wanting to offer commentary about Muslims in Australia, sport and religion provide her with a framework for life.

“When you have a belief in God, it humbles you and it gives you a grounding. I guess a good way of explaining this is to use road rules as an example. It gives us guidance. My belief in God does the same thing.”

Her mother, Feriyi Ramadan, a devout Muslim, confessed that she won’t push Susie to commit herself totally to her religion but she supports Susie in any decisions she makes in her life, as long as it doesn’t bring her any harm.

Her mother has never seen her fight. “I worry about her. It’s a rough sport.” Her father who passed away in 2024 used to watch all of her fights and was proud of what she accomplished.

Ramadan turned to boxing after a brief soccer career. “It was difficult in the early days, but I have earned respect from the boys. I now feel like I am going down the right road,” she said.

Respected boxing trainer, Ben Brizzi says he had reservations when he first saw Ramadan.

“When Susie walked into the gym you couldn’t help notice how small she was but she had this natural balance and took to boxing like a duck to water.

“She took a while to get used to the gym but eventually it became like a second home for her,” Brizzi remembered.

Boxing aside, Susie was clear about life outside the ropes. “I want to be a role model for other Muslims, men or women. Not long ago I visited a Muslim school in Melbourne and we spoke about achieving goals and having dreams. All I wanted to do was win a world title.”

Fighting as a professional for nearly fourteen years, despite the problems getting fights, Susie remains positive.

"I would fight any of the superfly weight world champions. Irma Garcia is the IBF Champion who we have tried to get to fight."

Mexican Garcia is a rugged champion with over 31 fights on her resume and would be a tough test for Ramadan.

Two of her four defeats were at the hands of Yasmin Rivas. The tough Mexican fighter has been her nemesis.

"We fought in Mexico both times and I felt I actually won the first fight," Ramadan recalled.

"The second time we fought we went 'at it' in the most dangerous place in the world. Durango is the centre of the drug cartel world. When we got there the promoter requested that we not leave the hotel because of the danger on the streets. It was scary but it's what I have to do to get fights."

It's well-known that a foreign fighter probably needs a knock out to win in Mexico. Dodgy judge decisions are commonplace. Perhaps her adversary is Mexico itself. Susie suffered her third career defeat losing a ten round decision to veteran Mexican fighter, Mariana Juarez in 2018. Juarez was having her sixth fight since April 2017. At the time it was Ramadan's first outing in twelve months.

Like women pioneers of an earlier age, female boxers struggle for recognition. Boxing commentator and founder of *Ring Magazine*, Nat Fleischer, argued that women boxers would have trouble bearing children if they fought. Based on no medical findings, Fleischer's comments perhaps reflected the attitude of times past, where women were confined to domestic duties in the family home.

It was suggested female boxers were prone to concussion,

didn't have endurance, and would be susceptible to breast cancer if they took blows to the chest. All unproven and fictitious.

Whilst attitudes have changed, women still only fight two-minute rounds with men fighting three-minute rounds.

Former promoter of Ramadan, ex Super Featherweight world champion, Barry Michael, said she should be seen as being one of the best fighters Australia has ever produced, irrespective of gender.

"She is a brilliant boxer. In my view she is the female Johnny Famechon. She has great defence, is a great combination puncher, and she can dig deep when she needs to. Her three losses in Mexico have been on points. I have watched those fights and reality says that she might have lost only one of them," Michael said.

Barry Michael is known as one of Australia's best fighters and is a good judge of boxing talent.

"It's difficult for her to get fights because she is very good and people don't want to fight her," Michael said.

"Over the past couple of years the Corona virus has held things up, but the fact is the title holders don't want to fight her."

More than a passing curiosity, professional female boxers are now ranked by all the main world boxing organisations. Susie fights in the Super Flyweight division in which there are over one hundred world-rated females, approximately ten percent of the number of male fighters in the same division. The growth of female boxing globally is remarkable, given that male boxing, bare-knuckled or gloved, has been around for centuries.

Boxing as a whole has its ups and downs, but the popularity of female boxing is a highlight in a sport that has had its fair share of black eyes.

When the bell signals the start of the bout, Susie's misgivings evaporate. She is quick, beautifully balanced, a study in non-stop movement and controlled aggression.

Like the scarlet pimpernel she is evasive and lightning fast. One moment she throws lefts and rights in front of her befuddled opponent and then in an instant, she stalks her from behind.

Long term fight fans stare open mouthed in disbelief. In a blurry haze, she punched in bunches. Her opponent looked rattled and confused. Punches bounced off her head and she couldn't do anything to stop her and it became obvious she just wanted to survive.

For a brief moment Susie was challenged. Against the flow of the fight, a random left hook smacked against her skull. The crowd gasped. Her momentum was halted briefly, almost like she needed a moment to collect her thoughts. And then she simply kept punching. Boxing afficionados nodded their approval. It was proof, she was tough enough.

Walking back to the change room after another win, Ramadan looks every bit a winner. Red faced, sweat-soaked and smiling from ear to ear, she is satisfied and so is the crowd.

In a brutal business, Susie Q continues to fight and the clock continues to tick, as she waits for that one big fight, that one big win, to finish her career.

Belinda and Jasmine Duarte (photo Western Bulldogs).

Belinda Duarte – An Indigenous History

Yurra Yurra man Robert Kinnear stared down the track, totally focused.

It was 1883 and Kinnear stood at the starting line of the famous Stawell Gift, the world's richest professional sprint race. As an Indigenous athlete, he shouldered the dreams of his people.

As he crossed the line in first place, he brazenly thrust his arms skyward and looked to the heavens. The crowd gasped. Such a raw display of emotion was totally out of character for an athlete. With the eyes of Australia on him, Kinnear's actions spoke volumes.

There was a time when Belinda Duarte wanted to emulate her great granduncle Robert Kinnear. She got close, and was a finalist in the women's Stawell gift one year.

As an athlete she won three women's Gift meetings on the tough Victorian Athletic League circuit and finished seventh in the Olympic Heptathlon trials. Her personal sporting pedigree was solid.

Like Kinnear, Duarte had grown up surrounded by discrimination. Belinda Duarte no longer runs but now goes about her work in the boardrooms of Australia, perhaps a tougher gig than the Stawell Gift itself.

It was 1983 and Belinda Duarte (nee Jakiel) was 10 years old. Just like her great granduncle Robert Kinnear 100 years before, she stared down the track. It wasn't the famous Stawell Gift but a local 100-metre race at a school sports carnival.

A boy taunted her, calling her a Boong. Belinda was stunned. She eyeballed the track. She knew what he was saying was wrong. It was demeaning and intended to hurt her.

Like her great granduncle she let her actions do the talking. The gun went and she ran like a hare. It was the fastest she had ever run. Her arms and legs pumped in sync and people stopped and stared. She was good.

She won the race easily. Like Robert Kinnear, her actions spoke the loudest. Walking off she didn't need to say anything to the boy, her win spoke volumes.

It's 2021 and 49 year old Belinda Duarte ponders the Doug Nichols round of the Australian Football season. Pastor Doug Nichols was an VFL footballer and the first Aboriginal Australian to be knighted. He was also Governor of South Australia and a pioneer for human rights.

She sits on the board of the Western Bulldogs and has played a key part in the clubs involvement in the round of football that celebrates Aboriginal and Torres Straight Islander cultures, and their contribution to Australian football

A fierce First Nations social justice advocate, Duarte has been a key part of leading social inclusion progress with the Western

Bulldogs and this year's guernsey.

Designed by former Bulldogs player Lindsay Gilbee, she is proud of not only the guernsey but the development and progress of the Indigenous round on the AFL calendar.

"I'm so glad to see this round has become a landmark event on the AFL Calendar. It's one of the biggest rounds as far as attendance goes, along with the grand final and the Anzac Day game," she said proudly. "We still have a long way to go but we are getting better and its getting bigger."

Duarte, a trained teacher and Wotjobaluk / Dja Dja Wurrung woman, has a long and impressive list of board appointments including the MCG trust and the Annamila First Nations Foundation amongst others. She has also been the co-chair of reconciliation Victoria and Deputy Chair of Responsible Gambling Victoria. She was the youngest board member ever appointed to the Victoria Health Board.

As the Inaugural director of the Korin Gamadji Institute at the Richmond Football club and the 2012 AFL Woman of the Year, Duarte has become an unwilling poster woman for Indigenous affairs. She insists she has fallen into leadership type roles and hasn't actively pursued them.

"Ever since I have been a little kid I have been nudged to be in leadership roles. Peers, the teachers and the ancestors seem to push me in that direction," she says. "It's almost like they grab me by the ear and say come on girl you go get in there."

Whether in leadership roles or not, Duarte is clear on her role in life. "I feel like I am a translator. Whether it's a sport context, education or boardrooms, I can see things and translate them for others to understand."

For the first Indigenous executive in the AFL, social justice and equity are important to her. She is CEO of Culture is Life, an organisation that focuses on the prevention of Indigenous youth suicide.

She asked me if I knew what the incidence of suicide was of First Nations young people between the ages of fifteen and twenty four. I didn't. It was double nationally and up to four times higher in certain areas than non-indigenous suicide.

Duarte gets a steely, focused look when she needs to make her point. Her body moves in the chair, she leans forward and points her finger.

"I stand up for communities that I am from. There is something that has compelled me to always give voice when something is unfair. I can see things that other people might not realise that is completely unfair.

"It is hard wired in my DNA because of acts of injustice and abuse that you have to just keep getting up and fighting for what's right."

A sense of fairness drives Duarte and she shoulders the responsibility well. You won't find her ducking from a battle.

"I do feel it's my sense of cultural responsibility. Considering what has happened to First Peoples in the history of our country. I will always speak up. I'll take action, even when it's uncomfortable," she said.

I asked what it meant to her to be an Indigenous leader, she responded with a question of her own, "Am I an Indigenous leader or a leader?"

It was a question that didn't require an answer.

A Ballarat girl, she has fond memories of growing up with her two sisters and brother. She is very good at telling stories and laughs hard when talking of her siblings. I inevitably laugh with her.

Her family are working class and she has old school country values. A result of her parent's morals, she says. A smile breaks across her face when talking about her family. She speaks of them a lot.

Her connection to her heritage runs deep. Duarte's mother is a proud Aboriginal woman and her father a proud polish refugee. When talking about her parents she softens. Tough and resilient is how she described them. Both parents did it tough. The admiration for her parents is obvious. Her father, a returned Vietnam veteran, passed away in 2005. Her mother and siblings still live in Ballarat.

She speaks of "Cuppas" around the table, the cold Ballarat Winters, and the things country kids did, that city kids didn't. She built cubbies, went tadpoling, yabbying and picked blackberries. She loved growing up in the country.

Other than her family link to Robert Kinnear, Duarte's third great grandfather travelled to England to play with Australia's first international cricket team.

Dick a Dick or Yanggendyinanyuk was part of the First Eleven of Aboriginal cricketers that took the field on Boxing Day in 1866. A nice touch, Duarte presented the newly minted Mullagh medal for the best player of the Boxing Day test in 2022. Appropriately, Gulidjan man, Scott Boland took home the medal. Sport was a rusted-on part of her family identity. "Sport was everywhere in our family," Duarte says.

"Mum was a softballer," Belinda said. "Everybody would

stop and watch her pitch because she was so good. Dad was conscripted to serve in Vietnam and his mentality and physicality were about being tough. He used to take us kids for runs in his gym boots," she remembered.

Belinda Duarte knew sport was a place she belonged, a place where she could challenge herself and not have to use words.

A mother of a 16 year old daughter, talking about family stirs deep feelings. Often during our conversation she stops to gather herself as the tears flowed.

"My family breathe life and purpose, they breathe reason, reality. They are what really matters. I will always say I love who I am of."

As much as Duarte feels the love from her family, she carries a sense of guilt as she straddles two worlds, one in Ballarat and one in boardrooms around Australia.

"Sometimes I get tired of being in these settings. I feel extraordinarily alone. I get exhausted by it and environments are set up to not hold people like me. Sometimes I just want to bail and not do it," she concedes.

"I feel like I need to get better for my family. I left home and my family are still there. Maybe I should have stayed." Her words drift off. Wiping the tears away, she stares at the floor.

Media veteran and friend Shelley Ware has watched Duarte develop over the past twenty years. The Yankunytjatjara and Wirangu woman, has a deep affection for her.

"I crossed paths with Belinda in the AFL space. She is a powerhouse. She just rolls her sleaves up and gets the job done. She never blows her own trumpet, she is modest, kind and very open to helping other people," Ware said.

Ware talked about Aboriginal people being focused on creating a better future for themselves almost as if it was an Indigenous edict.

"For Belinda it's about children and their future. It's at the forefront of her mind. The work she does with Culture is Life and her work around suicide prevention and kids."

A former panellist on the *Marngrook Footy Show*, Ware believes Australia is in a transition period concerning Indigenous history, and Duarte has been key part of that transition.

"The next generation of Indigenous kids coming up are amazing. They are savvy, understand their history and are simply awesome. Belinda has been good at allowing our younger people to believe in themselves."

Deeply sensitive, Duarte speaks about her heritage and social justice with passion. It means a lot to her. She has the uncanny knack of controlling her words when she gets emotional. It's a well-honed skill.

She takes long deep breaths to steady herself and chooses her words well to make a point.

She spoke of the massacres, racism, and the treatment of Indigenous Australians. She talked of the 26th of January and the effect of that day on First Nations people.

"The sentiment of the 26th of January is to acknowledge and celebrate Australia. For us as First Peoples, it's a day that recognises a moment in time that forever changed the fabric of our families and communities.

"I never looked forward to it. Growing up and hearing and

having conversations, it's awful. Every person in the country should feel good about celebrating a national day but for our mob generally we don't. It was recognised as a Day of Mourning in 1938 by Aboriginal people and it remains that."

With Aboriginal culture in Australia dating back 60,000 years, Australia has every reason to celebrate what is one of the oldest cultures in the world.

"I get really emotional about the grace and the love and the patience of our people. They should rightly be angered by how systems have treated them and by how people within the systems have treated them," she said.

Duarte's mother, aunty and uncle were part of the Stolen Generation. There were more tears than words in this conversation and she did her best to explain.

The Stolen Generation referred to the forced removal of children from aboriginal families between 1910 and 1970 by the Australian government. The Aborigines Protection policy from the late 1860s the late 1960s, decimated communities as Aboriginal people were put into missions and reserves. Families were torn apart.

Anger eventually replaced the tears and she took aim at those making decisions for Indigenous Australians.

"They took the opportunity away for me and others like me, to have the cultural information passed down to me in our language. The totems, the traditions, the land and the stories. Generations have missed learning about our own culture."

To understand more, I went in search of Indigenous history. Frontier Violence was commonplace. Spoken of in hushed tones, you will find stories of atrocities in official history books and mass killings were common. Genocide was first carried out by British soldiers in 1794 and killings continued up until the late 1920s.

The Guardian newspaper reported that more than 500 Indigenous massacres have taken place around Australia with more than 6000 Indigenous Australians killed. More were killed in this country than the total servicemen and women in wars fought by Australians offshore.

Entire communities disappeared overnight and Duarte declared that "there isn't one clan or community in Australia that doesn't have stories of massacres and abuse".

It's no wonder Indigenous Australians are hurting. Trauma is passed down through generations and has been found to influence DNA. In this way, younger generations aren't immune to the atrocities of the past.

All speak of healing. Healing from a past that has been ignored. Healing from massacres, the Stolen Generation, and from uncountable murderous injustices.

Australian First Peoples have a beautiful way of telling stories. Tales of the Dreamtime are passed down over generations. Songlines and knowledge systems, magnificent animals and stories of ancestral beings are shared. Yarns, thousands of years old, are told around campfires and involve celebrations and sophisticated dance rituals that preserve cultural practices and a way of life.

First Peoples have a unique connection with the land and it's for this reason that Belinda Duarte loves nothing more than camping around Dimboola and anywhere on country. It grounds her she says, and she isn't the only one. Its Wotjobaluk land. Country is intrinsically who she is.

"I need to be on country. I become focused and a better person. I think about the elders that came before me and it helps me."

Robert Kinnear died in 1935 and is buried in the Antwerp cemetery. Duarte has visited his grave.

Kinnear won the Stawell Gift with his hands raised to the heavens or as I have learnt, to Sky Country. Like her great granduncle, Duarte is raising her arms in defiance for her people. Her fight isn't on the track but in boardrooms around Australia, struggling for the rights of First Peoples in active resistance to the oppression of the past and living legacy of its impact today.

The last word in this story could be left with Yorta Yorta man Pastor Doug Nicholls.

"Australia is the only country in the world that has completely usurped the rights of its Indigenous people. The skeleton in the cupboard of Australia's national life, is its treatment of Aborigines. We have not had a fair deal. It was bad enough for us to lose our country but it's one of the saddest stories of modern times that we should have become outcasts in our own land."

Munich 1972–
The Haywire Olympics

Charlene Rendina has a long memory. So do Erica Hooker, Pam Ryan, and Judy Pollock. All four women represented Australia in the 1972 Munich Olympic Games.

Munich was dubbed the Cheerful Games by organisers. For Germany it was an Olympics to represent peace after the atrocities of the second world war. For 10 days it was just that. Large cheerful crowds, great celebrations and record-breaking performances were highlights.

It all went awry though. In one day of crazed madness, the Olympic movement was driven to its knees, forever staining a memory of not only the Olympics but of four Australian women who were there.

It was the perfect time of year in Munich. Summer had become Autumn and the warm days were followed by pleasantly cool nights. The flowers were in full bloom and Olympic and East German flags flew side by side on the spotlessly clean streets.

The Munich people were struck by Olympic fever as over 7,000 athletes from 121 countries descended upon the Bavarian capital. It was to be an athletic celebration of peace. Post the second world war it was an opportunity for Germany to highlight a new modern democratic society and a chance to move on from Adolf Hitlers 1936 Nazi Olympics in Berlin.

Security was kept to a minimum and any signs of weapons were well hidden. Surprisingly this included the athlete village, which had a perimeter fence but very little in the way of a police presence.

Purpose made for the Olympics, the athlete Village in Munich was a concrete jungle. A mix of high-rise apartments and smaller three level blocks. These days it's used as student housing.

The Australian team accommodation was split. The men were on one side of the village and the female Australian athlete rooms were on the other side and stared directly into the Israeli team rooms less than 50 metres away.

It was 4.35 am in the morning of the 5th September. Not a sound could be heard as the village slept.

It was dark when Eight heavily armed Palestinian Arabs wearing ski masks entered the Munich Olympic Village. Meeting little resistance they quickly pushed past the permitter fence and using stolen keys entered the Israeli team dormitory.

Meters away Pam Ryan, Erica Hooker, Charlene Rendina and Judy Pollock slept, oblivious to what was happening.

Shots rang out and two Israeli's were quickly slaughtered. Others were held hostage and some were tortured.

A militant Palestinian terror group called Black September demanded the release of Palestinian nationals imprisoned in Israel. The face of modern terrorism was exposed for the world to see.

Historically confined to the Middle East, a bloody feud between Palestine and Israel, that had beginnings in the late

'Sixties, was to be played out on an international stage.

For the first time, live television images of such an attack were beamed into homes around the world. Broadcast in real time, a billion people watched the drama unfold.

Black and white pictures were plastered across broadsheets and news bulletins. A now famous photo of a masked terrorist became the symbol of a tainted Olympics, an Olympics that changed the world.

I went to visit Charlene Rendina at her house in the Melbourne suburb of Eltham North. The 78 year old still looks remarkably fit. These days her fitness regime involves a daily walk, a far cry from the grueling training sessions required as one of the best 400 and 800 metre athletes in the world.

Like the perfect host she welcomed me in, offered me a cup of tea and we sat talking in her lounge room. The grandmother is very easy going, polite and smiles a lot when she talks.

Rendina had a remarkable athletics career. She was a Commonwealth Games Eight Hundred Metre gold medalist and dual Olympian.

The 1972 Munich Olympics was her first major international competition. In a remarkable effort, she made the final of the Four Hundred Metres and finished sixth.

A brilliant athlete, Rendina has also been good at keeping secrets. One secret she has kept for over 50 years. A secret so personally devastating that she hasn't wanted to think about it let alone talk about it.

She broke her silence the day we met.

Rendina's remembers the 1972 Munich Olympics like it was

yesterday. Her room in the athlete's village was a stone's throw away from the Israeli team quarters.

"I was from here to across the road." Rendina said pointing to her street. "We lived it and saw it. I saw him." She spat the words out. Her smile disappeared.

The person she referred too was the balaclava-clad terrorist known as the Masked Figure of Doom. It was a famous photo soon to symbolise the Munich tragedy.

"All the other countries were hanging out the window watching as he was parading up and down with a machine gun," Rendina remembered.

"We didn't know why they were there. We didn't know who they were targeting. We were just told to go back to our room and not watch."

The minutes turned into hours. The army descended on the athletes village, helicopters hovered overhead and armed vehicles blocked the exits. It was like a movie set. Rendina couldn't believe her eyes. Huddled together with her teammates, frightened, afraid and uncertain of what was happening, she wondered if she would see her family again.

Terrified, Rendina closed her eyes and pressed her hands to her ears to block out the sound of the helicopters. She wanted it to go away.

A planned rescue attempt was aborted when the West Germans realised the entire world was watching on television sets. After hours of discussions and negotiations an agreement was made.

The West Germans had agreed to fly the terrorists and their hostages by helicopter to an airfield twenty five kilometers west of the Olympic Village. It was 10pm on September 5th when the blindfolded and bound hostages were bundled into waiting buses by the Palestinian terrorists and taken to waiting helicopters.

German sharpshooters were positioned at the airport with orders to eliminate the terrorists once they arrived at the airport. The plan went horribly wrong and a bloody battle ensued. The Palestinians turned their guns onto the hostages and shot anything that moved. Grenades exploded and the remaining nine Israeli hostages were killed, along with five of the terrorists and a police officer. Three members of Black September were captured.

In total 11 Israeli nationals were killed. *The Age* newspaper in Melbourne ran the headline, Day of Blood and Tears. It was appropriate. For Rendina and others, the tears have lasted a lifetime.

"Some of them (the Israelis) were in the middle of competition," Rendina recalled. "You train as an athlete to represent your country and no one would have thought that anything like that would happen. It's supposed to be sport."

The day of terror was a rest day for athletes. Charlene Rendina was to run her final the next day. To reach the final Rendina had broken an Olympic record and was in the best form of her life. In her final she stared down at the start line not knowing if she would be shot. Were the terrorists in the stadium? Did anybody know what was going on? In the greatest moment of her life, she was struck with fear.

"I loved the games, because I ran my best, above my best really, but the other side of it was horrendous. None of us knew what was going on and we were scared."

Charlene Rendina posing for the Australian Womens Weekly *May 1972* .

Charlene Rendina on the left representing australia in the relay.

Above: Erica Hooker (nee Leigh·Nixon)

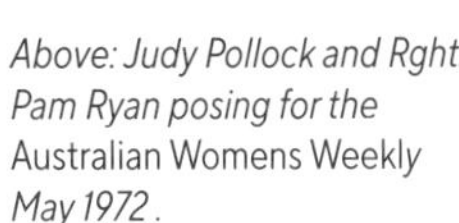

Above: Judy Pollock and Rght: Pam Ryan posing for the Australian Womens Weekly *May 1972 .*

Rendina cried and admitted she was sadder than ever.

"I am more emotional now than I was then, it was frightening. After we got back to Australia nothing happened. Our team managers told us to ignore what happened, to forget it and put it behind us? Can you believe that," she said. Her question didn't require an answer.

Mental wellbeing in 2022 is seen as being just as important as physical health and trauma is addressed with significant counselling and support.

Rendina felt she and the other athletes had been forgotten and it was a surprise when she said that nobody has ever asked if she was ok. "Not once has anyone ever asked us. Nobody, ever."

Pam Ryan, 86, who's maiden name was Kilborn, represented Australia at three Olympic Games, winning silver and bronze medals. With six Commonwealth games gold medals to go along with her world hurdles records,

Ryan is an all-time great of Australian athletics. Inducted into the Australian Sporting Hall of Fame in 2008 she described her experiences at the Munich Olympics as devastating, her lowest point as an athlete.

She doesn't want to remember anything about Munich and admits to being "still so upset that every detail has fallen out of my head."

Whilst many were affected, Ryan felt it more than most. Travelling around Europe in the lead up to the games she befriended Israeli hurdles coach Amitzur Shapira. He was travelling with an athlete in the lead up to the games.

Athletics is a lonely sport and the constant travel from

competition to competition and country to country, becomes a burden. The solitude can be soul destroying and friendships are hard to come by.

To find a friend so far from home was comforting for Ryan, They ate meals together, went on sightseeing tours, joked and laughed. It was a welcome relief and helped her navigate the lead up to the games.

Amitzur Shapira was tragically killed on the tarmac in the bungled attempt to save the hostages.

Ryan remembers being shattered by the news. She still struggles with the memory today.

"They were lovely people. The last time I saw him was the day before he was shot. It was devastating and I still don't like to think about it," she said. "He was my friend."

Ryan made the final of the Women's One Hundred Metres Hurdles, held the day after the tragedy. Two weeks before the Games she had equaled the World Record and was a favourite to take gold. Burdened with sadness, she didn't run to expectations and finished fourth.

"I just wanted to get away," she told me. "It affected my race for sure but I was devastated. I can't think of Munich without feeling bad. I still remember it when I see helicopters and hear the Popcorn song. That's all they played at the athletes' village. I hate that song."

Judy Pollock and Erica Hooker were two other women affected by the terrorist attack. Pollock was the Track and Field Captain of the Australian Olympic team in 1972. She didn't compete because of injury, but the former 1964 Olympic Four Hundred metre medallist has trouble forgetting the horrors of Munich.

"How can you forget something like that? You didn't think about this when it was happening but our family who were watching this back in Australia had no idea if we were alive or dead," she remembered.

It was the silence from team management that was hard to fathom. Its been a silence that has lasted an age. Like Rendina, 85 year old Pollock recalls the specific instructions to forget it when she returned home.

"It was almost like the fact people died and nobody seemed to care about it. They said nothing to us afterwards, nothing at all."

"We needed to talk to someone. It wasn't good and it's still not good."

For eighteen year-old long jumper Hooker, it was her first major competition and her first overseas trip. On the day of the attack she visited her mother and aunty away from the Olympic village.

"I got back to the village and didn't know what was happening," she said. "I was shocked."

Struck by the silence, Hooker likened it to a numbness that hung over the Aussie team. People spoke in hushed tones and an eerie subdued cloud hung over the athlete village. Confused and dazed nobody seemed to know what to do or say.

"None of us ever spoke about it and life went on after that day. I don't think it actually caught up with me until I went to a Munich exhibition in Melbourne sometime in the 'Nineties. That's when I lost it. I couldn't stop crying."

Hooker cried because of the trauma. The agony of that day lay deep within her body. Under instructions from team bosses the anguish had been left unresolved.

Now seventy three years of age, the mother of Olympic Pole Vault gold medallist Steve Hooker remains saddened and admits to needing help.

"It's had a huge effect on my life and how I have impacted my kids. I can't keep speaking to people about it without crying. The big thing is, we are practical and pragmatic people, and we should just deal with it, but it just doesn't go away. I probably need to speak to someone. I really needed some help back then."

In the days after the tragedy a memorial service was held to commemorate the slain Israeli athletes and staff. Every country and all athletes were invited.

Pam Ryan, Charlene Rendina, Erica Hooker, and Judy Pollock, along with every other female on the Australian track team, were forbidden from attending.

In line with the poor treatment of female Aussie athletes, only Australian male athletes were permitted to be at the service.

"I was so angry," Ryan recalled. "I wanted to go with the Australian men and just pay my respects and get some closure in my life. I actually knew someone that died. None of us women were allowed to attend. but that's how female athletes were treated back then. It was a horrible trip."

According to Kilbourn female athletes were an afterthought and simply filled the spots that males didn't take on the team.

"There was always double the amount of men and we were an afterthought, even though we won more medals than the men," she said.

Only 139 men and 29 women represented Australia across 20

sports at Munich. Times have changed and of the 472 Australians that competed at the Tokyo Olympics in 2021, 254 were female.

Eleven Israeli nationals didn't return home from the 1972 Olympics and four Australian women are struggling with memories of that terrible attack.

Perhaps the 'Seventies was a time when simply looking away and locking out memories made forgetting easier. It certainly wouldn't be that way today. Trauma is dealt with in a very different way and counselling and open discussion play a key part in healing. Mental well being is as much a part of an athlete's life as physical training and psychologists play a crucial role in an athletes support group.

It could be a sad truth that many Australians are silently coping with the traumatic effects of what was experienced at Munich in 1972.

Charlene Rendina, Pam Ryan, Erica Hooker and Judy Pollock are friends. They have each other for support but remain haunted by an Olympiad that was in many ways brushed away. It didn't need to be like this.

For these woman, and many other people, forgetting the 1972 Munich Olympiad has been difficult, but forgetting the tragedy that unfolded there has been impossible.

The Westerman Jilya Institute

The Westerman Jilya Institute was founded in 2019 by Dr Tracy Westerman AM following the heartbreaking loss of 13 Aboriginal children to suicide in the Kimberley. The Coronial inquiry found that children were continuing to die because of systemic failure and a lack of access to culturally competent services.

Driven by determination to make a change, Dr Westerman self-funded the Dr Tracy Westerman Indigenous Psychology Scholarship Program and pledged to #BuildAnArmy of Indigenous psychologists so never again shall a child die from a lack of access to services. Dr Westerman continues to volunteer her time with Jilya, logging 16,000 hours to date.

The Jilya model is an Australian first, providing not only funding to recipients but also significant wraparound support. Students are not selected based on grades; they are selected based on how much disadvantage they represent; how many gaps they have to close compared to others.

Scholarship recipients represent some of Australia's highest risk communities including Halls Creek, Cherbourg, Tennant Creek,

Derby, Walgett, Mt Isa and Alice Springs.

Since its establishment, the scholarship program has supported 79 Aboriginal and Torres Strait Islander people to pursue careers in psychology, achieving Australian record graduation rates in the process. Four in five students (79%) have completed undergraduate studies and gone on to commence postgraduate degrees compared to just 27% for all universities nationally, that's almost triple the national average.

The vision is to reduce Indigenous suicides, child removals, and incarceration by strengthening wellbeing and resilience in Indigenous Australians through culturally grounded, evidence-based mental health responses.

100% of donations made to Jilya are used for the Jilya programs. If you donate you can select what program area you wish the donations to go to. Any support no matter how big or small is appreciated and helps us continue with this vital work.

Scan to Donate